To our dear fri...
Bob and Jean.

Judy Lovins

The Redhead in the Mirror

Judy Horowitz Fenster Lovins

Running Quail Press, Inc.
Arizona, USA

For information, address Running Quail Press, Inc., PO Box 5274, Peoria, AZ 85385-5274.

ISBN: 978-0-9840331-6-4

Printed in the United States of America

First Edition

For purposes of discretion, the names of some of those who have peopled my life have been changed in this telling, and where two people have the same first name, I've changed one of them to avoid confusion.

CONTENTS

Beginning

A DIFFERENT KIND OF LOVE

"*Vilda chaya!*" Mother often shouts at me, which means wild animal. But look at me curled up quietly in the corner of the maroon plush sofa next to my family's Philco console radio, lost in my Saturday morning programs. Let's Pretend opens with music that makes me so happy I'll remember it all my life—*Da DUM d'dee dee dee, DUM d' dee dee dee, DUM d' dee, da DUM.* As the plots unfold, I especially love it when a handsome prince comes for the girl who needs to be rescued.

Let's Pretend is followed by Stars over Hollywood, whose stories move away from fairy tales into the real world. My all-time favorite story is Bright Victory, about a doctor who falls deeply in love with a patient he knows is going to die. He marries her without telling her what's in store and stays by her until her destiny comes to call. Sitting dreamily in my sheltered corner, I hope that when I grow up I will love somebody that completely.

I know that kind of love is different from what I feel now for my daddy and my big sister Roan. As for Mother, she's a fine lady who ar-ti-cu-lates her words precisely, as she learned in her childhood elocution lessons, and she wants Roan and me to follow in her carefully placed footsteps (never toed in or toed out). Peacock-proud of being born in America, she has a big, sophisticated English vocabulary, but when she's mad at me, she forgets all that and explodes in the gravelly Yiddish her parents spoke at home. When I feel trapped by her fury washing over me, I forget to love her.

THE PROPER DAUGHTERS

My namesake grandmother, Judith Libman, bore two sons in Russia before my grandfather Louis left them to sail to America and establish himself in Hartford, Connecticut. Among his first English words were, "Look in the basket." Employed to sell sundries door-to-door, he understood that if he didn't recognize the name of an item his customer wanted, he was to invite her to look for it in the basket looped over his arm. When he'd saved enough of his earnings, Louis sent for his family to join him. Judith handled their young sons Morris and Lou on the long sea voyage by herself, as other emigrant mothers did. As time went on in Hartford, she gave birth to Abe; my mother, Mollie; and then the baby of the family, Little Aunt Rose. Meanwhile, Grandfather rose from peddler to owner of the upscale Savoy Hotel, a well-spoken and widely respected gentleman known for his scrupulous dealings in his business and the community.

According to Little Aunt Rose, by the time she was born, her sister Mollie, as the youngest child and only girl in the family, was enthroned as the pampered little princess of the household. Both girls were trained to be admirable (if a bit snobbish) young ladies, proud of their respected family name carved high on a prominent building in downtown Hartford.

The two girls were quite different from each other.

Mother was short and pretty. Her slightly bent-bridged nose got along well with her high cheekbones, soft brown eyes, jet black hair, and an exotic brown mole just northwest of her top lip, set against an otherwise flawless complexion. Early on, she acquired a curvy figure that rivaled her face for attention. (The mole was removed in later life to safeguard against cancer.)

Rose grew up taller and bigger boned than Mother, with the same cheekbones making her angular features look stern. Her hair was auburn, her skin freckled. Because I had my aunt's coloring, if not her style, she was the visual link between me and the redheaded grandmother I never knew. As a little girl, I grimaced silently when my Uncle Morris, twenty years older than my mother, would fondly bite my cheek, less gently than he supposed, and call me *Mammaleh* because I reminded him so much of Judith.

While Mother remained the coddled, timorous daughter at home, Rose became an independent soul who in her late teens was already helping to manage the Savoy. When her father declined to accompany her on a tour of Europe, Rose went by herself.

Mollie's attempt to venture forth was not as successful. Upon graduating high school in June 1918, she, like many well-bred young ladies, heeded the desperate call for nursing students to replace the thousands of Florence Nightingales still deployed to war zones. Civilian hospitals at home were short-handed. With a suitcase full of stylish white uniforms bankrolled by her father, Mollie eagerly set off with a friend to train at New York's Beth Israel Hospital.

When she and her friend arrived, the flu pandemic was so rampant that no more hospital beds were available. The two young ladies were horrified to find patients lying on cots in the corridors. In the extreme emergency, desperate supervisors threw the untrained neophytes into the wards at once, where they watched one patient after another die. It took only a few days for reality to quash their idealistic dreams, chasing Mollie, her friend, and all those stylish uniforms back to Hartford.

After the war, a handsome young entrepreneur from Brooklyn began staying at the Hotel Savoy whenever he came to check on his family's local dress shop—part of a successful chain in Hartford, New York, and New Jersey. Also an American-born child of Russian Jewish immigrants, the middle of three brothers, Dan was a savvy New Yorker who could sell you the Brooklyn Bridge. He had the sparkling blue eyes of the Horowitz men, blond hair, a ready sense of humor and a talent for soft-shoe dancing. Grandfather Louie took a liking to him and invited him home to dinner. As Dan walked in the door, he smelled potato latkes frying, and when he learned that Mollie was making them, it was goodbye, Charlie! He sold himself to her, and they were married in 1926. Roan came along in 1928; I followed three and a half years later.

Little Aunt Rose married stout, big-hearted chiropodist Harold Blum, and when they weren't blessed with children of their own, they lavished their love on Roan and me. They started out in a home in Rockville, Connecticut, with a terraced garden where Roan and I loved to smell the flowers, watch the colorful butterflies, and catch grasshoppers in a bottle. Later, when they moved to Chatham Street in Hartford, they made their first-floor flat bright, fresh and inviting.

I loved to visit there. Lying prone on the carpet under the elegantly framed copy of van Gogh's bright Sunflowers that dominated the room, I'd choose from the Sears, Roebuck catalogue open in front of me the dresses, shoes and jewelry I'd buy if on my own. For lunch I rapturously devoured the heavenly bacon Aunt Rose cooked for me that was forbidden in my mother's kosher home. In later years, in the abyss of my adolescence when I'd made myself and my mother most miserable, my aunt would invite me to walk over to her place just a block away. She'd hug me, empathize with my complaints, and fuss how, if she were my mother, she'd treat me differently. She plied me with bacon and calmed me down. Her home was a welcome haven, her hugs a needed lifeline.

Because Rose and Harold had so much to give, they adopted a child of their own, but the outcome was tragic. Baby Billy was a behavioral challenge from the day they brought him home. At the age of three, he was diagnosed as so mentally disadvantaged that it was deemed best for him to live in a facility equipped to care for such children. The Blums unselfishly let him go, and under the aegis of a trained staff, Billy became a happy child, a fan of baseball and Roy Rogers (whose name he pronounced incomprehensively but was understood by our family). Rose and Harold never abandoned him. They brought him home on alternate weekends, fed him his favorite foods, took him to favorite places, and enveloped him in their love. I was included in many outings with Uncle Harold and a delighted Billy, sitting in the car, licking ice cream cones as we watched the afternoon train go by and thrilled to its rousing steam whistle.

Aunt Rose, true to her own upbringing, not only kept Billy well dressed and groomed but painstakingly schooled him in manners until he became a perfect gentleman. Without a child permanently at home, she filled up her life with social service, dedicating herself more and more to B'nai B'rith as she rose through the ranks to preside at both the local and regional levels.

My Libman grandparents, who both died before I was born, would have been proud of their two proper daughters.

LEFT BEHIND

It's 1935. The doctor is on his way to our house to give Roan and me shots against that dangerous whooping cough. Though I'm only four years old, I know what a shot is—the doctor sticks a fountain pen in your arm and shoots in some ink. I really, really don't want a shot, but I'm too young to choose what happens to me.

Roan and I are each sitting on one of the wide ledges on either side of our front porch, waiting for the doctor to get here. We aren't talking a lot, each gazing across Greenfield Street at the Weaver High School football field, thinking our own scared thoughts. When the doctor's car finally pulls up, I look sideways across the porch and I can't believe my eyes! Roan is gone! Everyone asks me where she is, but I can't tell them; I never heard her leave. They look for her a long time. Finally, when she can't be found, the doctor gives me my shot and goes on his way. I'm so happy he doesn't use a fountain pen but a thing he calls a needle, even though it's a lot bigger than what Mother uses to darn Daddy's socks with on the wooden egg with the handle.

Later in the day Roan shows up and claims that she forgot about the doctor's visit and just happened to choose this time to visit our Big Aunt Rose. That's the wife of Uncle Morris, the biter. She's shorter than Little Aunt Rose but is called Big because she's older. Morris and Big Rose don't live too far away, but I'd get lost if I tried to go there by myself.

I feel let down that my sister stole away without warning me or inviting me to go with her. She just left me to face the big, bad wolf by myself. But I'm glad that I got the shot and happy when she gets hers later, 'cause that awful whooping cough is going around killing children like us.

Another day I get really mad at Roan, but she asked for it. I'm standing in front of the only toilet in our rented flat and have just lowered my panties to sit when she plows through the door with her playsuit already down, slides under me and plunks her fanny down first. In a flash I turn around, get my head behind her and sink my teeth into her bare shoulder blade. Her screech of pain and accusing me brings our parents on the run to see my teeth marks in her skin. Her shoulder is turning purple, and I'm scared of what I've done. Am I really a *vilda chaya*? Oh, you should hear the yelling! For a couple of days I can tell Mother and Daddy are sorry they ever had me. Then Little Aunt Rose and Uncle Harold bring me a new doll almost as big as I am, hug me, and plead with my parents to love me again. Mother and Daddy listen and get nicer. But the main reason I'm so relieved when my big sister's back finally becomes a smooth pink again is that after all, she is my best friend.

I spend half of every day in low kindergarten down the street. My teacher's name is Miss Crayon. There's a girl in my class named Caroline who is definitely not a friend. In a roomful of toys, the only ones Caroline wants are those I already have in my hands. As soon as she sees me playing with something, she drops what she's holding, comes over to take the doll or toy away from me, and starts playing with it herself. I find something else I like, but as soon as I pick it up, here comes Caroline to take it from me. She does that over and over. I feel like crying, but I don't cry. Instead I complain to Miss Crayon. She says in a prissy voice, "We must learn to share," and turns away. She never talks to

Caroline about it.

I'm surprised to learn that sharing means someone can take something away from you without being invited. From now on I will always hold tight to my belongings and my space unless I choose to offer them. What's mine is *mine*, and you'd better not use or take it without asking me!

One day our class is going to walk to the park. We are lined up in two rows and are told to hold the hand of the person in the row across from us. Guess who's across from me? Caroline! Mother says we mustn't hate anyone and may only say we *intensely dislike* them. Boy, do I intensely dislike Caroline, and I have to hold her hand all the way to the park! Ugh!

Well, we're moving to Blue Hills Avenue pretty soon, and I will go to a different school there.

TRAPEZOIDS

I flunked scissors in kindergarten and still can't cut straight. Even trying to cut on a line drawn between two measured dots, I somehow always fall off it. I suspect I may be as bad at measuring as I am at cutting.

So it was that the "number facts" I had to make for learning addition and subtraction in first grade emerged from the cardboard sheet not as neat rectangles but as trapezoids. Had a uniform set of printed flash cards been available then, it might have saved my nascent self-esteem. But elastic-banded together, my handcrafted version made a pretty sorrowful pile.

Since I was also a failure at keeping a tidy desk, the haphazard cardboard conglomerate kept getting lost in the depths of my domain. One day in second grade when I again held up the class searching for the infamous deck, my frustrated teacher decreed before all my peers that I must go back to the first grade classroom to make a new set.

Back to first grade? Oh, the humiliation! I jumped up, and standing rigid next to my desk loudly informed Miss Walsh, "My father knows the cops in West Hartford, and he will report you!"

Wherever did I come by such a notion? I doubt my father knew anyone even vaguely connected with police anywhere. West Hartford was an affluent town to be aspired to, but my family lived in Hartford proper, and Daddy did business in East Hartford. I guess I just decided to aim high.

Although I didn't receive any additional sentence for my insubordination, my face got hotter and hotter as I was marched to the first grade classroom, seated at a child-sized table in the corner and provided with a new supply of cardboard, crayons, and the dreaded scissors while the younger kids looked on agog.

My deficits being what they are, the new set of number facts once again emerged as trapezoids but were accepted. Back in my own classroom, I made darned sure to keep track of where I put them when arithmetic lessons were over.

Thoroughly chastened, for the rest of my life I've maintained the exemplar of an efficiently organized desk at school and at the office. But in deference to Miss Walsh, let's just keep the condition of my home office a secret between us, shall we?

FREEING LILLIAN

I was born in October 1931 into the crises of two Great Depressions—the world's financial crash and my mother's postpartum adjustment.

The obligations of the three dress shops owned by my father, L. Daniel Horowitz, in partnership with his father Sam and brother Larry, were discharged in bankruptcy. But my parents couldn't abide leaving their creditors holding the bag. Dad went to work for Metropolitan Life, and luckily he was as gifted a salesman of insurance as of ladies' clothing. Yet in spite of his making good commissions, our family lived frugally over the next decade until every dress shop creditor was paid the last cent of the legally forgiven amount.

Roan tells of her bewilderment at three-and-a-half years old watching her promised Precious Baby Sister come home from Hartford Hospital in the arms of a white-clad nurse while Mother was carried to her bedroom on a stretcher. Mother's nerves were shot, and although she could manage her children okay after the nurse left, she clearly needed help in the house.

She found it at Long Lane Farm, a Connecticut reformatory for wayward or neglected underage girls who had committed or were in danger of committing minor offenses, including playing hooky from school or choosing very wrong friends. When not in detention, the teenagers were paroled out to reputable homes as live-in housemaids until they were twenty-one. It was the only help my family could afford, and if the girls listened, my mother could be a life-changing help to them in return. But sometimes her message was so loud that it was hard to hear.

From my earliest years, even when we couldn't afford a phone in the house or a bicycle for Roan and me to share, we had such a live-in "girl", whom we weren't allowed to call a "maid". But that's what she was. On Blue Hills Avenue our maid slept in the playroom where my three neglected dolls lay in their carriage. More importantly, our prized blackboard hung on the wall there, waiting for Roan to impart some new knowledge to me or for me to make my own mark. Not a very private space for the room's unlucky resident.

It didn't seem to me that being in our home was any better than being in detention. There were strict rules for the girls to follow; they couldn't go out alone or have anyone in, and my mother's cleaning and behavioral standards were lofty. The maid did not sit at the table with us for meals; she ate alone. Occasional routine visits by the parole officer, Miss Mecum, to check on her charge were unsettling (although it gave me the opportunity to collect that dignitary's signature in my autograph book).

Almost never did a girl's parents come to take her out for a day, and she had no opportunity to make friends. No contemporaries to talk to, only the four of us. Roan and I were well aware of what she was missing, because on the rare evenings when our parents went out and left us in the care of the maid, we'd have a rollicking time sitting on her bed, listening agog to prison tales. Matron "Old Lady Eastburn" often came "pussyfooting down the hall" to catch someone in a misdeed. Fellow inmate Philomena sometimes walked on "milk-bottle legs," other times on "piano stool legs." One night a group of girls stole and ate a whole can of peaches from the kitchen without benefit of an opener. Oh, if our parents only knew the stories we heard!

These resident babysitters would let us stay up way past bedtime, perform plays on the living room's pre-Depression Oriental rug without removing our shoes, or make fudge in the kitchen—always too soft but as delectable as only forbidden food can be. For a small bribe from my minimal allowance, one of the girls even let me have the fun of ironing my father's sprinkled breast-pocket hankies or some table napkins. To test if the iron was ready, she taught me to wet my finger on my tongue and touch it to the sole plate, drawing it away instantly. If my saliva sizzled, the iron was hot enough. I'm proud to say I never burned a finger or a hankie.

Since the maid wasn't allowed out on her own, pipsqueaks Roan and I chaperoned her to the Lenox movie theater most Saturday afternoons. It was a mile's walk from the house. In the lobby Roan and I bought two Sugar Daddies packaged together for a nickel, and those all-day suckers lasted through the newsreel, short subject, cartoon, Green Hornet episode, previews of coming attractions and into the first of a double feature! The maid used her own allowance to buy herself a box of Good & Plenty candies. We three sat together.

For most of Mother's young charges, the valuable things she tried to impart were drowned out by her stern demands. Once I watched her follow the maid on all fours, re-wiping baseboards when the girl's efforts failed to satisfy her meticulous standards. In my deep scowl could be read my silent vow, *I'll never be like that!* and I've kept that promise. Best leave your white gloves at home if you come to visit my house.

When instruction and warnings failed to bring a girl's performance or attitude up to snuff, Miss Mecum was called and came to take her back to the bosom of Old Lady Eastburn. Only one parolee ever reached her maturity in our home. What a celebration when Miss Mecum came to tell Betty that she was a free woman, and her father arrived to take her home! Betty had been with us for several years, and she fervently thanked my mother for all she had taught her beyond housekeeping—she was taking away a redirected life and a value system she had never known before. Although I continued to disapprove of Mother, I now saw her in somewhat of a new light.

Most of the Long Lane girls were benevolent to Roan and me. When we lived on Greenfield Street, Daddy took the spindle back and tray off my outgrown brown wooden high chair to create a high-legged stool. There I sat, watching in the mirror as the earliest remembered maid combed goo into my long coppery hair, twirled it into curls, and wrapped them in rags for overnight. The next morning, unwrapped, I thought I was as pretty as Shirley Temple!

But mean Martha scared the bejabbers out of me. Once when I was still only four, Roan and I were left alone with her. Though I had no idea what my misdeed of the day was, Martha picked me up and plunked me down on the kitchen table next to a chunky, double-handled pottery urn splotched with brightly colored flowers. Planting her black-haired arms stiffly on either side of me; she leaned her face into mine; pulled back her lips to bare her teeth; and ground out, "Jody! You're so BOLD!" I hated the way she distorted my name whenever she was mad at me, erasing my existence. I didn't know what *bold* meant nor what she meant to do next. Trapped by her menacing presence, I turned my head and fixed my eyes on the bright pottery next to me, hoping maybe that was the bowl she was comparing me to. I believe I suffered no more than that verbal terror, but the urn, sitting on the bookcase in Roan's family room since Mother passed on, still whispers *bold* every time I pass by.

And I guess I was. Once when Mother herself called me *vilda chaya* for the umpteenth time, I stunned my father by hollering back at her, "What do you think you are?" I wasn't afraid of *her*. And she wasn't afraid of me.

I did like our young maid Lillian. One Sunday morning on Blue Hills Avenue, I heard a commotion under the playroom window, and when I looked out I saw Mother talking with two uniformed policemen below! I ran downstairs and looking up, saw a twisted bed sheet hanging out of the second-story window. Lillian had knotted one end to the radiator just inside and slid down the sheet to make her getaway before Mother discovered her room empty.

I thought *Yay, Lillian! You're free! Keep going!*

But one policeman pointed out that the sheet was too short to reach all the way to the ground, and one footprint on the slightly muddy ground beneath it was deeper than the other.

"She twisted her ankle when she jumped off," he concluded. "We shouldn't have trouble catching up with her."

My insides lurched like a Down elevator and my throat tightened. *Oh, no!* I cried inwardly. *Please don't let her ankle be twisted.* I began praying for a clean escape.

We heard nothing for the rest of that day, but when I came home from school on Monday, my mother told me, "They found her and took her back." So what good was prayer? Our getaway had failed.

Later I began inching toward my own freedom. On entering high school, Roan was let off the hook, but I still had to walk the maid of the moment to the movie every Saturday. I protested to Mother, "No friend will go with me because nobody wants the maid along."

Since the film changed overnight, Mother offered a compromise. "Take the girl on Saturday, and you can go with a friend on Sunday." Now, there *was* a grand escape! A whole weekend in another world!

But my joy was soon compromised. Finally clear of Depression debt, my folks bought a beach house in Westbrook, Connecticut. That summer Mother announced that Roan and I were now old enough to make our own beds, clean our own rooms, and help around the house. No more parolees in the playroom! Since we'd been spared, and indeed not allowed those chores all our lives, I had no idea how to capture the dust between the toes of a lion's-claw couch leg or get the upright vacuum's puffed-up belly under a bed. We needed the rigorous training the maids had been given, but strangely, Mother assumed we'd absorbed it all by osmosis and taught only by stern *post facto* criticism. I felt like Lillian.

Inside the new cottage was a naked flight of dark wooden stairs, which I had to back down one step at a time while brushing beach sand and dust into a dustpan. I loathed every corner of every stair that resisted giving up its cache of gritty grains. In addition, sometimes I had to help Roan wrestle the living room rug over a clothesline, where she beat the sand and dust out with a heavy hand-held instrument of steel loops. Oh, why had we ever grown up?

Back in our flat in Hartford, another *bête noir* awaited me. Mother loved house plants and potted them in unusual containers like a discarded plastic pocketbook and an antique cloisonné bowl. But for her mass of small-leafed red and green coleus, Dad made "ferneries", long wooden boxes that were filled with soil and plants and sat atop the radiators under the dining room windows.

Even as the coleus flourished and multiplied, the steam heat from the hissing radiators dried out a multitude of their leaves, which fell down behind the cast iron coils. Expletives (in English) distinctly unbecoming to a lady roiled through my head while I dropped flat on my stomach and poked a long-handled brush under the radiator to retrieve the crackling brown corpses. Wonder no more why you never see that live plant you gave me as a house gift!

Mother's favorite transplants into odd curios were various species of cactus with stabbing needles. Without blossoms, I thought they were so ugly! I never dreamed that one day I'd live far from Mother amid gorgeous large, vividly blooming cactus on a magnificent desert.

I'd survived to the age of fifteen when one Friday, Rita from around the corner suggested we take in the movie at the Lenox that night. I no longer had a maid to walk, and my classmates were by now attending movies after dark. But when I told Mother what Rita proposed, she said no, I was too young. Always too young for this and too young for that, but old enough, all right, to crawl in after those damned coleus leaves! I'd had enough! My plan hatched quickly.

"Well, then, can Rita and I at least go to Sabbath services at the Emanuel?" The synagogue was only a few blocks short of the theater. Same route, same nighttime, but this trip was approved.

When Rita and I got to the Emanuel, we kept right on going to the Lenox to see The Jolson Story in glorious Technicolor. While finally snatching the freedom denied our maids, I trembled inside. Again and again I swiveled my head, shifted my eyes, checking that nobody I knew would spot me there and report back to Mother. I thought *This must be how Lillian felt when she was running on her twisted ankle.* Never have I enjoyed a movie less.

But when I got home and Mother asked "How were services?" I didn't hesitate.

"We didn't go to services. We went to the Lenox." Looking straight into her shocked face, I continued, "The next time I go to the movies on a Friday night, do you want me to tell you I'll be at the Emanuel, or will you want to know where I really am?"

Mother capitulated. I was free to go to nocturnal shows thereafter, and she need not wonder where I was.

Lillian, you are avenged!

BLUE HILLS AVENUE

When we left Greenfield Street, my family rented the upstairs six-room flat of a two-story stucco house in northwest Hartford. It was the last step up before stylish West Hartford, where some of my Sunday school classmates' families had already bought single homes as the Depression gave way to war.

At first I thought the outside walls were called stucco because small shards of shiny colored stones stuck out of the rough white base material. These were easy to pry loose and became the jewels Roan and I sold each other in our imagined store on the downstairs porch running across the front of the house.

Three or four wide wooden stairs descended from the porch to the cement walk leading out to the public sidewalk along Blue Hills Avenue. Playing Stoop Ball alone or with a friend, I'd launch the rubber sphere against the painted grey steps and try to catch it on the rebound. Here I also sat to wait my turn at bouncing the ball on the walk until I failed to cleanly throw my leg over it. Colored chalk to draw Hopscotch grids and keys to adjust roller skates were the tools of the trade of our childhood. My friends and I jumped rope singly or Double Dutch, using one or two ropes or jumpers at a time. We played Giant Steps—my favorite was the umbrella step, twirling around while moving forward. But I deemed Red Rover a contact sport suitable only for boys.

One door on the porch led into the first-floor flat of the Altschuler family; inside the other door a grey-carpeted flight of stairs led up to ours. On those stairs I spent many hours arranging two-dimensional paper dolls either by myself or with Roan, fastening their beautiful clothes to their cardboard bodies with paper tabs and acting out scenarios with them as characters.

Roan had long Veronica Lake blonde hair, a sweet smile, and a slim figure. The time came when she was being pursued by so many boys that she had no more interest in paper dolls. But as I got older, I loved designing more clothes for them to wear and houses to live in.

From the landing at the top of the stairs a French door led out to our square, open front porch, where I felt cozy reading even bundled up under a winter sun. In milder weather, Roan and I played school out there. I was never much interested in lifelike dolls, but I loved it when Roan sat me at a feigned desk and imparted all she'd recently learned in her classes. Because this generous and talented teacher was four grades in front of me, I was always ahead of my peers.

But one day in an unteacherly fit of irritation, as I sat inattentively fingering a gift I treasured—a silver-tone ring set with an impressive glass stone—Roan snatched the ersatz diamond and flung it clear across the pitched first-floor roof that bordered the porch. It landed in a rain-filled gutter. Heartbroken, I almost sailed over the broad wooden porch ledge to retrieve it, but navigating the pitched roof looked too dangerous even for my rash instincts. And so the cherished jewel was lost forever. But I have forgiven my sister The Ring Toss, as she has forgiven me The Big Bite.

The back stairs of the Blue Hills house bypassed the Altschulers' kitchen door and ran up to a landing between our flat and our enclosed back porch. On laundry days Mother knelt on the floor in the kitchen, struck a wooden match on the scratchy side of a rectangular matchbox, and lit the pilot at the bottom of our cylindrical gas water heater. Our maid had already brushed off the pale blue crystals that stuck to its inside coils after our last baths. When the water was hot, Mother plugged in our round four-legged, open-top washing machine and did the laundry. After the rinsing, she warily fed everything through the attached wringer—that pair of rubber rollers notorious for also grabbing fingers, long hair, or boobs (Mother's were ample) that got too close. She dropped the wrung-out items into a basket, which she carried out to the back porch. There she leaned out a sliding window to hang them on a line that reeled in and out on a pulley. She pinned the items to the line with a mouthful of wooden clothespins that had no springs but looked like two long legs joined with a knob at the top. Occasionally helping Mother in winter, I'd reel in flat white bed sheets frozen into stiff squares that crackled if I tried to fold them before letting them thaw.

On the landing between our kitchen and the porch was another door that always stayed mysteriously closed. Behind it more stairs led up to the attic, which our pleasant, elderly landlords, the Davises, had converted into living quarters for themselves. I wondered if the housing authorities knew that a third family lived above us. Both the Davis children were grown and gone, and the parents, though both stocky, were so quiet that we were hardly aware of them ourselves...except that Roan claims she could hear through the ceiling the sound of Mrs. Davis making chopped liver.

Since their daughter and daughter-in-law were both named Bernice, it was lucky that the Davises had always endearingly called their daughter "Boonkie". Because Ira's wife was "Bunny", we had no trouble discerning who they were talking about. Sometimes when Boonkie or Ira and Bunny came to visit their folks, we enjoyed a brief friendly chat.

One day I ventured upstairs to visit the parents. At

first sight of their quarters I could only hope that they couldn't read my face. Although they owned the house I lived in, the attic this elderly couple occupied wasn't even partitioned into separate rooms! As I sat talking with them, I was almost overwhelmed by the concentrated heat collected up under the roof. Before air conditioning, our own flat could be stifling in summer, but I wondered how our landlords could live in their virtual inferno! Could they not afford to forego the rent on one of the floors below and move down to greater comfort? Why didn't their children insist on it? *Maybe,* I told myself, *appearances don't always tell a whole story,* and as an afterthought...*especially when it's none of my business.*

Round-faced, bespectacled Michael Altschuler on the first floor was several years younger than I and an only child. We sometimes played together. Because his father, Arnold, worked in the toy department of Fox's, Hartford's major department store, the extra bedroom in their flat was a treasure trove of playthings. There was even a movie projector, and whenever Arnold Altschuler brought home a new episode of the black-and-white children's cartoon, Felix the Cat, I'd be invited downstairs to watch it.

Though his young age limited his skills, sometimes Michael joined me in athletics on the Jungle Gym my father had installed in the back yard. Then I invented a game called Tunnel, where we crawled under each other's spread legs. This allowed me to satisfy my curiosity over what lay under his loose shorts, until Dora Altschuler looked out the window, noted that I slithered under her son *on my back,* reported it to my mother, and ended my scandalous premature sex life.

It was with the Altschulers that I took refuge in 1938 when I walked home in a storm from my school two blocks away and found our unlocked flat empty. No one thought it necessary to lock doors, but it was unheard of for Mother not to be home for us. Roan wasn't back from school yet, and I don't know where the maid was. I was uneasy as the insistent wind picked up force, and I became really alarmed when Mother's carefully tended clay flower pots were blown off the upstairs porch ledge and smashed on the walk below. The Altschulers were kind enough to take me in till my worried mother got home, delayed by what turned out to be a hurricane. All those toys in Michael's playroom succeeded in keeping me so well distracted that I barely looked up when she arrived.

The storm had also slowed Roan's progress home from school. She was climbing up the Holcomb Street hill on crutches, her leg having been broken when a furniture truck struck her as she was crossing Blue Hills Avenue. Later Roan, Mother, the maid and I stood at our front window and trembled as the gale slammed down the venerable elm tree across the avenue, just missing the house behind it as it fell.

My father didn't get home that night but was stuck on the other side of the swollen Connecticut River, where he'd been selling insurance policies and collecting premiums door-to-door. He bunked in with Mother's cousins in Glastonbury. In the morning Mother took us downtown on the trolley, where a kind gentleman lifted me into the bed of his pickup truck at the top of the Trumbull Street hill to watch Daddy being rowed home from East Hartford. His car came home when the river went down.

Once our cousin Murray came to visit us from Florida. His family had emigrated from Willimantic, a thread mill town neighboring the University of Connecticut, to manage a hotel on the glamorous Miami Beach newly dredged out of the Florida bay. But he was still a small town boy. A half hour after we'd all gone to bed, Murray tore out of his room wild-eyed, asking in a tremulous voice, "What was that? What's happening?"

"What was what, Murray?" Roan asked.

"That loud noise! Sounded like thunder or a big explosion!"

We'd heard no such thing and looked at each other in puzzlement. What could it be? When Murray pointed out front, it dawned on us that he'd been awakened by a trolley rumbling by on its accustomed night schedule. Chuckling, we explained the big, bad noise and got him back to bed. Living on the main line for so many years, the sound of the trolley was almost a lullaby to us.

As we grew older, so did the house, and it needed some care. The renovation of the downstairs front porch began one June, just before we were to leave for a month at the beach. A careless construction worker left a pried-off old board lying on the front walk, with a long rusted nail sticking straight up from it. Graceful as always, I bounded out the door and down the stairs without looking, and my foot, clad in a paper-thin-soled moccasin, came down hard on that nail. Yow! The full length of the nail imbedded itself in the sole of my foot, firmly anchoring the board to it. I was alone. I silently hopped to the stoop, sat, and tried to pull off the board, but it wouldn't budge. Only after several minutes of painfully rotating that board did I finally twist the nail out of my foot.

By now a Girl Scout trained in first aid, I knew just what to do. I don't remember any blood. At least I got upstairs without staining the carpeting, thoroughly doused the wound with hydrogen peroxide from the medicine cabinet, fashioned a gauze and tape bandage, and donned different shoes. By now we had no maid, nobody else was home, and I decided it was unnecessary to tell my parents because we were going to the ocean the next day. There my foot would be repeatedly soaked in salt water—the perfect antiseptic. I must have been blessed by the tetanus god, because the rusty nail puncture never got infected, and I never had to worry the folks. I was grateful that Mother, who was my Scout leader from Brownies all the way up to Juniors, had mentored our troop through our first aid badge.

Several years later, with their first fledgling flown

away to college, Mother, Dad, and I were ejected from our nest. As the Davises aged further, Boonkie, Bunny, and Ira sold the house to our familiar shoemaker, Mr. Ucello. Under rent control in effect since the war, he was only allowed to evict a tenant if he wanted their space for his own family. Apparently the sweltering attic held no attraction for them; they wanted to live on the second floor. My parents, taken aback, moved our family's belongings to a newer first-floor flat on Hebron Street, away from the trolley line and only a block from Little Aunt Rose and Uncle Harold's Chatham Street place. Roan and I packed up our memories and took them with us.

THE SLEUTH SISTERS

On Blue Hills Avenue, Roan and I not only share a room, we share a bedtime. My bed is on the other side of the dining room wall, but nightly after lights-out I cross our rug to be welcomed into Roan's domain against the window. She lies flat on her back with her feet in the air, her knees bent. I position my stomach on her feet and spread my arms. When she straightens her legs, I'm flying. Whee!

This airline completes many flights, but when the last plane lands, Roan and I proceed to our stake-out. On the first floor of the house next door live four career-girl sisters: Sylvia, Sadie, and the twins, Eva and Belle. They seem very glamorous to us. From our spies' perch upstairs we can see right into the window of their lighted sitting room. And since they never pull down their shades, we easily keep tabs on their activities. These consist mainly of the silent reading of books, muted conversations, suspicious disappearances into the kitchen, and sudden reappearances with unidentifiable snacks and a continuance of communication too quiet for us to pick up on.

Then one summer night, catastrophe! Sylvia is lying reading on a daybed just under their open window. Suddenly she raises her eyes, looks straight up at us and calls out, "Why don't you girls just mind your own business?" We are outed! And thus Blue Hills Surveillance, Inc. is shut down forever...almost.

I guess we're not so effective anyway. When Mother and Daddy entertain company, they all eat dinner in the dining room on the other side of the wall from my bed, and then the women go to a folding table in the living room to play Mah Jongg, and the men play Pinochle in the kitchen. There's a door that's never used from just past the foot of my bed into the dining room. One company night, as usual, I'm lying on the floor in my pajamas with my ear to the space under that door. I hear talk around the dinner table about a couple who, like all our parents' friends, are a courtesy aunt and uncle to us kids. I hear that the wife is going to travel somewhere while the husband stays home with the children. I really like these people and am so distressed that I blurt out from my cover, "Is Aunt Laura getting DWARFED?" The entire dining room bursts into laughter, and I learn that she is not *divorcing* Uncle Hank, and that I must be a more discreet detective.

Soon I see how a master sleuth operates. Upstairs from the career girls lives a real old couple, Mr. and Mrs. Manley. Although their windows are directly opposite Roan's, they turn out the lights and go to bed early. They're no fun to watch. But first Mrs. Manley dies, and then her husband dies. The Saturday afternoon an auction of their property is held in their flat, our mother joins us at Roan's window. Part way into the sale when the auctioneer holds up the next item, we hear a loud "OH!" from Mother, and she vanishes into thin air. The next moment we see her materialize in the Manley's flat, and after a brief chat with the auctioneer, here she comes up our front stairs holding a pretty china plate. Too bad I don't pay more attention to it, because very likely when I grow up I'll be serving company of my own on an unidentified plate my mother sprinted up and down two staircases to acquire at auction.

A young couple moves into the Manley's flat. We think they'll be more fun to watch until one night the mister comes to his refrigerator for a snack...stark naked! This time we pull *our* shades and Blue Hills Surveillance, Inc. goes permanently out of business.

THE HOUSE ON COLEBROOK STREET

Mother's best friend is Jessie Elovitz, who lives around the corner. As with all my parents' friends, I would automatically call her "aunt", but Jessie's sister Blanche is married to Mother's brother Abe, making her almost a true relative. All my short life I've been such good friends with Jessie's son David, born just a month after me, that early classmates tease us in singsong, "I know David's girlfriend, I know Judy's boyfriend." To set things straight, David tells the kids we're cousins.

"What kind of cousins?" they ask suspiciously, and David invents the term "cruller cousins" because, he says, the connection is twisted.

We're lucky kids. Mother and Aunt Jessie both love to read. Every Wednesday evening they walk the mile to the branch library on Albany Avenue and bring home books for themselves and their children. Daddy lets Roan and me stay up to see what treasures Mother has brought us, and we start reading right away. Wednesdays are red letter days.

David lives with his parents, older brother and sister, and Impy, a black and white toy terrier, in their own two-story Colonial brick house just across Blue Hills Avenue and around the bend on Colebrook Street. The Elovitz home is a magical place! In the large, airy basement is a folding clothes-drying rack which, when collapsed and turned on its side, turns into an airplane on which David is the pilot and I the stewardess, serving to imaginary passengers the meals I procure from the storage alcove in the corner of the Elovitz basement. In their attic is a crystal radio set that David has made with his father, Uncle Sam, and we can hear snatches of a few limited broadcasts on it. Better than that is the sound effects kit with items like red cellophane to crinkle for the sound of crackling fire and rubber cups to be walked upside down across a wooden bench for horses' hooves. We add some dialogue and are stars of our own radio program!

On the dining room table David and I often play a board game called Philo Vance after a popular fictional detective. While we play, Impy sits quietly at our feet. Once I watch David climb on a chair to change a light bulb over the table and coming down, almost step on his beloved dog. Shaken by the near miss, his eyes fill with tears. It's the first I know that boys can cry.

Living so nearby, David and I sometimes walk together down the two blocks to Holcomb Street School, later fondly renamed Sarah J. Rawson School to honor our principal. The autumn after graduating Rawson, we start walking together the mile along Blue Hills Avenue to Jones Junior High School. But David's legs have grown longer, his feet larger, and being of the shorter persuasion, I must scurry to keep up with his Seven League Boots. Soon I give up and share my morning journey instead with Eudy, my friend directly across Blue Hills Avenue, whom I tease about her slower hip-swiveling gait. David strides to school with some guys more his speed.

By winter David and I have formed a small new circle of friends, and four of us just fit in a row on his toboggan as it flies down the snowy hills of Keney Park. We all hang onto each other's waists and, laughing, roll off the toboggan in a bunch each time we near the bottom of the incline. When we've had enough of the bone-chilling cold, we walk back to Colebrook Street for hot chocolate, kindly served up by Aunt Jessie.

Uncle Sam owns an appliance store, and in 1948 he brings home one of those new television sets. Now sixteen years old, I'm invited one day to watch that TV with Aunt Jessie while nobody else is home. It's on a low table in their master bedroom. She's set up an ironing board near the bed and is standing pressing the family's laundry while I sit on the floor. Together we watch the only programming so far available—a boxing match that, with the newborn technology, looks like it's being fought in a snowstorm. Although we can just barely make out the punches, we remain riveted in dismay to the spectacle of Sandy Sadler capturing the world featherweight title from Hartford's own Willie Pep, right in Aunt Jessie's bedroom!

There are some folks I just like to be in the same room with. Aunt Jessie, with her soft voice and kind ways, her round, smiling face and brown hair pulled back in a bun, is high on the list. That afternoon with her is to be cherished.

ON BEING PUNISHED

Uh-oh, I've done it again. Upset Mother. She's yelled at me, peppering her tirade with Yiddish words she'd be ashamed to admit she knows in English. As the harsh guttural sounds come crashing through, her exploding final consonants sound more like a spitting cat than a lady. Now she's crossed the dining room and gone into the master bedroom to pull out of their mahogany bureau one of Daddy's leather belts to strap me with.

Oh, don't be concerned! We've done this before, and I've already positioned myself on the far side of the formal rectangular table that sits in the middle of the dining room. When she comes out of the bedroom, she'll chase me round and round that table brandishing the belt, but both of us know she'll never catch me. I believe she doesn't mean to. When we're both out of breath, she'll go back to the bedroom, return the belt to the drawer, and warn me never to repeat my latest sin.

As punishment goes, I prefer this little circus over a longer tongue-lashing or, worst of all, the droning, endless lecture by Mother, Daddy, or—oh, save me!—both of them on how to behave. I have trouble keeping eye contact during those sessions and secretly check the watch Grampa gave me for an earlier birthday. I think my parents want to kill me with boredom!

But then, you know that mahogany bureau? It's part of the same set as the dressing table onto which Mother used to lift me so that she could more easily put her arms around me when she called me her *kotchkie*. If I was her little goose, I knew I couldn't be all bad, and her arms around me told me that I was loved.

I KNEW WHERE I WAS

Although both of my Libman grandparents had died between Roan's birth and mine, I was lucky enough to still have Grampa and Gramma Horowitz to love. They lived in an apartment on Avenue U off Ocean Avenue in Brooklyn, New York. To get there before the Merritt Parkway was built, Daddy had to drive us from Hartford through the city of New Haven, Connecticut into New York. If we got slowed down behind a New Haven trolley lumbering along the center of the street under its overhead wires, the trip could seem interminable. Further on, a stretch of New York's Riverside Parkway went by Grant's Tomb. At that point the fearfully jumbled traffic I saw from the back seat of our car made me wonder, *When I grow up will I ever be able to drive safely through this madhouse? If I can, I'll be a real pro!*

Since getting to Brooklyn took half a day, we always went on the weekend and slept over at my grandparents'. With limited space in their apartment, I slept on two living room armchairs touching each other face-to-face with a sheet stretched taut across both seats. I got a kick out of being the only one small enough to fit in such a funny accommodation.

Morning brought a special treat—great Uncle Frank's flapjacks! His wife, Aunt Ethel, was Grandma's sister, and they lived close by in an apartment on Avenue T. Roan and I would walk there and be welcomed with doting smiles and warm hugs. Ushered into the kitchen, we loved to watch Uncle Frank pour his secret batter into the skillet, brown a pancake on one side, flip it into the air and catch it in the pan to cook the other side. And were those pancakes yummy!

On the way to Avenue T we might meet one of two special vehicles in the street. The ice delivery man let us retrieve frozen small chunks from the back of his truck, and we savored those cold, slippery morsels on our tongues. But more exciting was the brightly colored carousel mounted on a flatbed truck that brought its joy from neighborhood to neighborhood. One of our adults would have given us each a dime to pay for a ride. With beaming faces, we'd clamber up on beautiful jeweled horses that carried us amid flashing bits of mirrors and fanciful paintings round and round, up and down to the exhilarating music of the band organ.

On a hot summer day my family might take the trolley to Coney Island to swim or to enjoy the boardwalk's full-size merry-go-round, bumper cars, and other fun rides. It was at Coney Island that my father was accosted by the beach police. Attitudes had been loosening up, and Daddy had left off the grey knitted vest that came with his maroon wool swim trunks and webbed white belt. Almost as soon as we set our blanket on the sand, an enforcer appeared and warned Daddy that he must immediately cover his shamefully bare chest. Attitudes may have changed but the rules hadn't.

(Does anyone want to join me today in a movement to bring back the vest? To protect innocent by-drivers from assault by the Ugh Factor when a grossly overfed bare belly spills down over a bicyclist's waistband? Or, for that matter, from the Yum Factor when a well-disciplined torso suddenly distracts an impressionable lady from her steering wheel duties? These are downright safety hazards!)

Once after Gramma died, Grampa took Roan and me to Coney Island by himself, and after going on several rides with us came to The Cyclone. He didn't know what it was,

but he was tired, ready to sit down, and just watch us have
fun. He judged we were old enough to go on alone,
promising to hold onto any safety bars, and he would meet
us at the exit.

"Oh, no, Grampa," we cried, "It won't be fun without
you."

Well, it's hard for grampas to resist little girls, and so
after much coaxing he bought three tickets and settled one of
us on each side of him behind the bar that held us in the car.
How were we to know that The Cyclone had been built to
shine as the largest and most thrilling roller coaster in the
world? After the breakneck side swings and heart-stopping
dives down and around the track, all three of us thanked
heaven that Grampa had relented and come with us for
reassurance! Although, to tell the truth, we sensed that he
was more terrified than we were.

Sometimes Uncle Larry, Aunt Sarah, and cousin Big
Lois came from their apartment on Bedford Avenue across
from Dodger Stadium to see us at our grandparents'
apartment. (Just as in Hartford Little Aunt Rose was actually
taller than Big Aunt Rose, so in Brooklyn Big Lois was
shorter than younger cousin Little Lois, daughter of Daddy's
kid brother Eli. There was a big age gap between Uncle Eli
and his older brothers, and somehow we never saw much of
his family.) If Big Lois came with Roan and me to Uncle
Frank's, the three of us, after filling our bellies with
flapjacks, would go down into the basement. There among
other intriguing storage items we'd look for the bedspring
standing vertically on end. One of us would pull up a chair
and straddle the spring, plucking the coil "strings" of this
make-believe harp while the second one waved her hands to
conduct an imagined orchestra, and the third applauded
appreciatively. Then we switched roles for the next
symphony.

Aunt Ethel and Uncle Frank Lieberman had two
grown sons, Gilbert and Larry, their daughter Ruthie, and

before long a son-in-law, all of whom made me feel special. Ruthie was married to Benjie Aronow in her parents' apartment, and I was entranced with the wedding. The best part of it all was that I adored both the bride and groom.

I had never heard of a bride clad in anything except white, but Ruthie owned a dress shop and was wise in the ways of fashion. She wore a floating pale blue gown as romantic as a fairy tale...and BARE FEET! Shortly before the wedding she'd been stricken with athlete's foot and that day was unable to wear shoes. Standing ready to proceed down the hall of the apartment to where her groom awaited, each bare foot rested on a square of white paper. As she lifted one foot for her first step forward, a bridesmaid picked up the freed paper and moved it to the spot where that extremity would land. The procedure was repeated with the other foot and for each step down the hall, using only the two squares of paper. Such quick efficiency fascinated me, and happily Ruthie's unshod appendages in no way diminished the lovely illusion of the pastel princess.

Benjie was a sweet man, with only pleasant words emanating from behind his well-groomed bristly mustache. After he heard Aunt Sarah call me by my first and middle names full out, as she often did, he nick-named me Judy Lou the Funny Name. In laughing retaliation, I called him, not very originally, Benjamin James the Funny Name.

On a visit to Brooklyn shortly after Ruthie's marriage, Grampa invited me for a walk to her shop. I may have been around six years old. As we moved among the bustling throngs on the busy Brooklyn sidewalk, I suddenly realized that Grampa was not next to me. I looked around but didn't see him anywhere. Oh, well, I thought, I'd been taken to Ruthie's shop once before and remembered that it was just down the street from where I was standing. I decided to continue on by myself. There was only one obstacle between me and my destination—an intersection mad with jockeying automobiles. Noting many people standing waiting to cross the street at the traffic light, I melted into them and figured that when they stepped off the curb it was safe for me to go with them.

Once on the other side, I was halfway down the block when I heard a very frightened voice calling my name. I turned around to find my distressed grandfather running toward me.

"Where are you going?" he gasped.

"To Ruthie's," I answered calmly. "I didn't see you, so I thought I'd meet you there. Where did you go?"

"I just stopped for a minute to look in a store window. But you crossed that busy street by yourself!"

"Oh, no, not by myself, Grampa. I went with the other people on the corner."

One relieved grandfather hugged me to his chest and made me promise never to do such a thing again. Then we proceeded to my cousin's shop exactly where I knew we'd find it.

What goes around comes around. When I was grown and our own daughter was four years old, my husband and I took her to the circus in Hartford. After we surrendered our tickets, I looked up in the crowded entrance, and our Susie was gone! With trembling voices we called "Susie! Susie!" We twisted this way and that, our hearts pounding for an eternity before we spotted her among the crowd not far away. As I ran to her and clutched her against me, she coolly assured me, "I wasn't lost, Mommy. I knew where I was!"

At that moment I truly understood the look on my grandfather's face all those years ago in Brooklyn, New York.

A HANDFUL OF HAY

Mother was the idea girl behind family travels, and Daddy made it all happen, though he always characterized himself as "just the chauffeur." I'm told that even when I was a mere infant, he rigged a hammock above the back seat of the car for me to lie in while Roan sat between them in front, and off we went on little day trips to places Mother suggested.

Whenever we chanced to pass a truck piled high with square hay bales, Mother would reach out her passenger window and snatch a few strands of hay to hold. Now sitting in the back seat with Roan, I thought that was a dangerous thing to do. But Mother claimed that it brought good luck, and it was such a happy surprise to see our usually perfectly behaved lady up to mischief!

Mother knew another harbinger of good luck. If the weather became overcast, she told us, "Look up at the sky. If there's enough blue to make a pair of Chinaman's pants, it won't rain." We rarely had cause to dispute that wisdom. In later life I heard from other families that rain could be fended off by a Dutchman's pants, and finally, any old pair of pants, which greatly improved the odds.

Because Mother loved black-eyed Susans, we often stopped by the roadside to pick them. On one trip the whole family got so carried away that we filled the car's entire back seat and floor with Susans, forgetting to leave room for Roan and me! We had to bail out a bunch of those flowers before we could continue on our way. My sister favored Indian paintbrush ever since learning about it in Girl Scouts, but we only picked the first few of those we saw and then simply pointed and yelled, "Paintbrush!" as we rolled by other clumps.

One of our favorite destinations was McLean's Game Refuge in Granby. There we found a gentle little wooded mountain to climb, some horseshoe pitching pits, a croquet field, and a brook floored with smoothly rounded rocks. It was too shallow and ice cold for swimming but perfect for Ro and me to wade or sit in to cool off. After we ate Mother's packed picnic at the brookside table, Daddy often worked a crossword puzzle. He let me help with the everyday words and taught me some *esoteric* standbys of the *cognoscenti*. I learned both crossword and jigsaw puzzling very early at my father's side, and he is often right there with me today when I'm having fun with one or the other. (Roan's and my storehouse of words can be equally attributed to Mother's extensive English vocabulary, which fortunately far outran her colloquial Yiddish.)

One summer we took a trip to Cape Cod. We stayed at the Lighthouse Cabins in the town of Sandwich. The free-standing one-room accommodations, built around a central court, had rudimentary kitchens in them, but we had to cross the court to reach the common bathroom. During the night I woke Mother with the news, "I have to make a wee." Even in summer, once the sun went down it was teeth-chattering cold in the pitch black courtyard. While Roan and Daddy slept, Mother cracked open the door, took one breath outside, and quickly pulled me back in to the tall kitchen sink. She instructed me to drop my pajama bottoms, hoisted me up to teeter on the high rim and held her arms around me as I relieved myself. While I stole back to bed, she washed the sink as quietly as she could, and at breakfast in the morning nothing was said about the nippy nocturnal excursion we never took.

Outdoors on our picnic table, Mother lifted the orange juice out of our blue pebbled aluminum ice chest and took cutlery and dishes from the old suitcase Daddy had fitted out with straps to hold them. He unfolded the supports of our camp stove, lit the can of Sterno beneath it, and cooked eggs for breakfast. Conversing with other families doing the same, he related that I liked to sing. Then nothing would do but that I perform for them. Surrounded in that central court by a kind audience, I stood and sang my theme song, Pennies from Heaven. When they applauded and showered me with compliments, my self-image rose a notch—I was more than just a "little pisher."

Later in the morning, clad in swimsuits, our family laid out a blanket among the dunes of Cape Cod Bay. On this beautiful summer day, the sun was out full, the sky pure blue, the sand warm. We wasted no time running to the water's edge. SHOCK! With the first dip of toe into frigid ocean, our startled blood retreated like a turtle pulling its head inside its armor. Roan and Daddy spun around and headed back up the beach, where they fell to their knees and began building a sand castle worthy of a travelogue.

But Mother and I defiantly forged ahead and holding hands, immersed ourselves in the taunting sea beyond a submerged sand bar. Rising as one figure, we stood with clenched teeth, hugging tight to share our little body warmth, and laughed at the more timid half of the family. When prudence whispered that there was no need to prolong our victorious stance, we ran shivering out of the water and up the beach to swaddle ourselves in towels before admiring the architectural partners' emerging masterpiece. But that impressive edifice was no bulwark against the advancing tide, and before too long it was half dissolved, its creators deflated. That was our cue to pack up and seek warmer waters.

At lunch time we watched lobstermen further along

the shore pull up their pots and spill their crimson catch into boiling cauldrons on the pier. When our number was called, we collected our cooked critters and sat with our legs dangling off the pier, dipping chunks of the delectable delicacy into melted butter before offering it up to our overjoyed taste buds. There are no lobsters more heavenly than those eaten off paper plates on the spot where they're first brought out of water!

Dessert was always a couple of swigs out of the bottle of Fletcher's Castoria that Mother carried in her purse when we traveled. But that day was so much fun that we even forgot about the Castoria.

It must have been Mother's stolen handful of hay that invited fortune's benevolent smile.

THE SHOPPING TRIP

I name all my clothing. My Mrs. Levine Dress, a gift from one of my parents' distant friends, is royal blue with white buttons in big scallops down the front, a white Peter Pan collar, and puffed sleeves. Though I love the dress, I've outgrown it, and it's a happy day when Mother says it's time for a new one. She and I board the trolley, with its woven straw seats, on Blue Hills Avenue at Colebrook Street and alight at the corner of Main and Pratt Streets. In downtown Hartford the stores, theaters, and restaurants are strung out one after another along the sidewalks on Main and its cross streets.

Our first stop is the Society for Savings, the bank where Mother withdraws as much cash as she thinks we'll need for our purchase. I'm upset that she signs the withdrawal slip as Mrs. L. Daniel Horowitz, as if she's just an attachment to Daddy. I'm always going to use my very own first name, even when I'm grown and married.

In the dressing rooms of Fox's and Brown Thompson's I try on clothes with the help of friendly salesladies who handle the buttons and zippers or bring me a better size or color. When we decide on a dress, Mother hands money to the lady, who tucks it with the sales slip inside a metal cylinder with fuzzy ends and a little door in the middle. She closes the door and puts the cylinder into a vacuum tube that sucks it up with a *thunk!* into pipes that meander across the ceiling into the business office on a higher floor. The change that's due comes back by the same route.

In the shoe store, the salesman sits on a low stool in front of my chair, removes one of my shoes, and tells me to stand on a wide metal ruler that shows what length and width I need. He gets several boxes from the back of the store and comes out to sit on his stool again. I place my foot on the little ramp that slants down from his seat, and he puts a new shoe on it and laces it up. When I stand up, he presses his thumb on the end of the shoe to make sure my big toe has room inside. I walk around, and it's fun to look at just my foot in a little slanted mirror at floor level. If Mother likes the shoe, the salesman puts the second one on my other foot and I stand on a platform in the fluoroscope, which shows a light picture of how my bones fit inside them.

I'm praying that we do better than last time, when Mother insisted on buying ugly brown shoes that looked like a boy's, with reinforced toes to last longer. I begged and cried in the store and never wanted to take the hated things out of the box when we got home, but I had to wear those humiliating boy's shoes till I outgrew them. Imagine a small girl like me praying for bigger feet!

When we're done, since Mother hasn't spent all the money she withdrew, we return to the bank to put the rest back into the account. Then we stop for ten-cent Cokes at the luncheonette in Sage Allen department store before heading home.

There are controls at both rounded ends of the trolley car. At the end of the line the conductor goes down the center aisle and slides all the backrests to the front of the seats so they're now facing the opposite direction. He takes up his stand at the other end of the car, which is now the new front, and rolls up the sign that shows where the trolley is going. We board the one that says Blue Hills Avenue and without having to turn around, it heads back home.

I'm so excited to have something new to replace my Mrs. Levine Dress and new shoes sitting neatly on the closet floor! I can't wait to wear them to school tomorrow! But I should know better. I've forgotten that we're never allowed to take the tags off our purchases until Mother is sure we're going to keep them. Everything has been taken home "on approval," and if Mother changes her mind, she'll phone the store and their big delivery truck will stop at our house, pick up the item, and the store will send her money back. Sometimes for as long as a month, I lie in bed every night and stare at the treasure I can see in the open closet, hoping it will really be mine after all. The elation I feel at the start of a shopping trip is always crushed by the terrible suspense at the end. Will there be a big disappointment?

When I run my life I will be sure of my purchases before I leave the store. Tags will come off new things the instant they're out of the bag.

SHABBOS*

In our kitchen on Blue Hills Avenue stands a four-legged white Tappan gas stove with the baking oven rising vertically to the right of the waist-high surface burners. Every Friday at sundown, my mother stands in front of the oven, sets a pair of tall brass candlesticks on top for safety, and inserts two three-and-a-half-inch white candles into them. From the time I'm little, I drag a chair to the side of the oven and stand on it so that I'm level with Mother and the candles. We cover our heads lightly with clean dish towels, and Mother uses a wooden kitchen match to light the wicks. Together our hands circle above the flames three times. We are to light the candles at sundown, but we're not allowed to create fire once it's dark and the Sabbath has begun. To be on the safe side, traditionally we kindle them while it's still light but cover our eyes so that we can't see that the sun is not completely down. As the flames flicker unseen, we recite the Shabbos prayer in Hebrew and English:

"*Bohruch ataw Ahdonoy, elohaynu mehlech ho'olum, ashair keedshohnu b'mitzvosov vitzeevawnu l'hadleek nair shel Shabbos.*

"Blessed art Thou, O Lord our God, king of the universe, who has commanded us to kindle the Sabbath lights."

No matter if we were at odds before, in this one moment Mother and I share a bond as warm as the candles' flames. Just as we have encircled them with our hands, love encircles us. For that moment we become one woman, all women.

Although my family is not otherwise strict about observing the Sabbath, not everyone has adopted modern interpretation. One heavily overcast Saturday morning when I'm in my ninth grade religion class at Emanuel Synagogue, the natural light is so dim that I'm straining uncomfortably to read my textbook. I get up from my chair, go over to the wall, and flick on the overhead light. The whole class lets out a shocked "Ohhhh," and then I remember that on Shabbos strict observers do not create anything, including light. To rectify my error, I lift my hand to flick off the switch, but another chorus of gasps stops me. Destroying light would also be a transgression.

I turn to face the class and gently tell them what my heart tells me: "I really don't believe that God wants us to endanger the precious sight He gave us by reading in the dark." I am fourteen years old and it is the beginning of my apostasy.

But I will always carry with me the warm feeling of being blessed when I kindle the Shabbos lights with Mother.

*My family used the Ashkenazi (Eastern European) pronunciation of Hebrew. In 1948 when the State of Israel was created, the official pronunciation was declared to be as Sephardic (Western, Spanish) Jews spoke it. Thus *Shabbos* became *Shabbat*, and *bas mitzvah* became *bat mitzvah*. Out of nostalgia, the blessing over the candles is here transliterated the way my family spoke it in my early years.

BACK YARDS

In spring a strange little gypsy woman may suddenly appear uninvited in our Blue Hills back yard. She's armed with a sharp tool we view suspiciously until she digs it into the grass and pulls out dandelions by the roots, dropping them into the cloth bag she carries. Roan and I are afraid of her dark presence, but our father explains that the neighborhood is happy to be rid of the weeds and the gypsy is happy to have free makings for soup and wine.

But now we have no wispy dead dandelion heads to blow into the wind or dandelion stems to weave into jewelry. These activities are more fun than placing buttercups under our chins to see if the yellow color reflects up and reveals that we like butter. Or pulling daisy petals to see if "he loves me, he loves me not," though at our ages we have no idea who "he" is.

Another visitor to our yard is the man who regularly empties the in-ground garbage can with the green step-on lid. Pee-yew! We don't want to be around when he comes!

At the end of the driveway, blackberry bushes grow on the side of our detached garage. We love to eat the sweet berries right off the bush and bring a supply of them to Mother to serve with sour cream for dessert.

Inside the garage, Roan and I rehearse a puppet show that she's writing. We plan to invite Hartford's Mayor

Spellacy to Opening Day, but somehow the script never gets finished, and only my trio of dolls ever sees the incomplete performance.

Tied to the garage door on school days is our honey-colored, floppy-eared puppy, half cocker spaniel and half spitz. We've named her Happy after one of the Seven Dwarfs because she's small and always wagging her tail. She's tied up so that she can't reach Mrs. Altschuler's low-hanging laundry and soil or tear it with her playful paws. But Happy is perfectly content to sit calmly in her apple green, spindle-backed child's rocking chair and wait for us to come home for lunch.

We've been seen safely across the intersection of Holcomb and Cornwall Streets by our friend the WPA crossing guard, and at the top of Holcomb Street we cut across a couple of back yards to be greeted by Happy. When she spies us, she wiggles all over and runs the full length of her rope. We scoop her up, hug her, and bring her upstairs, even though Mother's afraid she'll get something dirty up there.

We immediately turn on the radio to hear what's new with Sister Ruth, Stella Dallas, and Our Gal Sunday. We need to know *Can this girl from a little mining town in the West find happiness as the wife of a wealthy and titled Englishman?* Lord Henry had better be good to our Sunday!

Returning from lunch one bitter cold winter day, I'm caught leaving the sidewalk and cutting across a corner of the school grounds to get inside faster. Because I've forgotten that my evil feet might tear the grass roots under the wet snow, I'm sentenced to stand outside, shivering, for an eternity before I'm allowed into class. That memory will always smart. It's worse than the time I had to stand in the front of the room, facing my classmates with my first and last wad of illicitly chewed gum stuck on my nose. At least then I was warm.

Next door to our house in a one-family brick home

live the Zaccagninos, who grow grapevines along the chain link fence separating our driveway from their property. The oldest son has my father's name, Dan. Second son, Pete, is a fireman, and Roan and I think daughter Rose is so sophisticated in her business clothes, perfect coiffeur, and painted fingernails. They are all kindly attentive to their two young neighbor girls.

On one occasion we have cause to be monumentally grateful for the presence of the Zaccagninos—we owe them my father's life! During a summer thunderstorm Daddy's sitting in his ribbed tank top undershirt at our kitchen table. Because the flat's so hot and the rain is falling straight down, he hasn't closed the window beside him. All of a sudden we hear a tremendous crash and see bricks go flying off the chimney next door. That chimney has intercepted a bolt of lightning headed straight for Daddy!

On the other side of the Zaccagninos are neighbors whom I've never seen. Roan and her best friend Phyllis have permission for the three of us to climb the apple trees in their back yard mini-orchard. One tree is especially easy to get into because the trunk forks off early into low branches, and we each claim a home on one of them. Then we visit back and forth among our branches, graciously entertaining each other with imaginary tea parties.

Looking down from our hospitality tree, I see clusters of enchanting violets scattered widely through the grass. Indeed, many of the lawns lining Blue Hills Avenue all the way to Westbourne Parkway are dotted with the lovely deep-purple flowers. For a short time those lawns also host tender little lavender-and-white Mayflowers. When I leave this carefree childhood and adolescent storm clouds gather in my soul, violets and mayflowers on my walk to school will bring me a welcome peace.

DADDY

While Mother was wracked with phobias, Daddy was afraid of nothing except maybe Mother. He knew how amazingly simple displeasure could turn a loving, well-bred woman into Mount Vesuvius.

Though a wiseacre who liked to make people laugh, my father would often lift a beautifully manicured hand to gently stroke my hair. He said it was the color of a shiny penny and sometimes called me by that nickname. As he himself went bald, he patiently let Roan and me comb and re-comb the few hairs that still floated across his head.

He was quick to encourage and slow to criticize. Watching me work at the kitchen table with a set of cutout wooden letters and put two V's together for a missing W, he called me "resourceful." I glowed at his praise and often took sustenance from that kitchen tableau.

Once when Daddy handed a beggar some money out our car window, Mother demurred, "He'll just spend it on liquor."

Daddy replied, "I'm giving it to him because I'm thankful that I'm not the one doing the asking." I liked him for that.

He spent hours in his well-equipped basement workshop making bookcases, shelves, and wooden toys for family children. I was warmly accepted into his sanctuary. Within the whir and whine of his electric tools and banging hammer, it was a quiet refuge from Mother where we could share a wordless silence brimming with love. When he finished a project, I felt privileged to sweep up the sawdust.

During World War II, many men and women came from as far as Maine in the north and Alabama in the south to live in East Hartford and work at Pratt & Whitney making aircraft engines. Lots of them became Daddy's clients. Although they wanted the policies Dan Horowitz sold to ensure that at the time of death there'd be money for their burial, many tried to duck out when "Mr. D" came to the house to collect the ten-cent premium. Daddy made us laugh when he described ringing one policyholder's front doorbell and immediately running around to meet her sneaking out the back door. Or the client he called Missus Sheez O'Clock, who told him in her foreign accent to come back at 6:00 p.m. but was never home when he did. By returning at random times, he managed to keep her policy from lapsing.

But to the majority of his clients Mr. D was more than an insurance man; he was a trusted friend of the family. They would call him at home at all hours for personal advice or to moderate a spousal spat over the telephone. We were so proud of him! The DePietro family, favorites of his, had him bring Roan and me to their farm to ride their pony. They even hosted a whole Day at the Farm for my Brownie troop.

Every night after dinner, Daddy had to complete a form itemizing the day's premium collections. I was thrilled when he began letting me help him record and add up the long columns of figures. He taught me tricks and shortcuts my school teachers never mentioned that enabled me to add a column zip-zip-zip. I learned not only about math but also about my father. The total at the bottom of the form had to match the total of coins and bills he counted out on the table. If we were as little as one cent off, he wouldn't throw in or take out a penny to make it balance, but we'd start all over with his dictating each policyholder's payment and my writing it down. Then we'd add up the columns again until we found the error, no matter how long it took. I was filled with admiration for him.

My father would never think of talking with his mouth full while dining, but away from the table his words were most often spoken around a Phillies cigar. I liked the smell of cigar smoke, but I didn't enjoy watching his tongue roll the wet stub from one corner of his mouth to the other. It looked so much cleaner when he held a cigarette between his fingers as he talked, and more elegant when he smoked a pipe. It wasn't often that there was nothing between his lips but his teeth.

He didn't walk, he hustled, and I guess I learned my unfeminine gait from him. He cleaned his dinner plate in record time, and I copied that, too. He ordered an egg salad sandwich at his friends' luncheonette every day while working Over East, and often when Mother was about to set a plate of kosher meat on the table for supper, he'd declare, "You know, I'd just as lief a couple a eggs." He ignored his diabetes and Mother's pleas to stop noshing, and he succumbed to a heart attack at the age of sixty-two.

By that time I had lost his love, and I was numb. It was almost comforting to realize that I was no longer the only one left behind.

HAPPY

One day when Daddy climbed the stairs to our flat after working Over East—SURPRISE! Cradled in his arms was a honey-colored, soft-haired puppy he'd been given by one of his clients. Ignoring Mother's ferocious frown, Roan and I danced for joy. Though not pleased about the unexpected new child, Mother let us keep her. She went about potty-training Happy by covering the kitchen linoleum with newspapers, removing one page at a time and rewarding her for peeing only on the sheets that remained.

The little one learned her lesson too well. One day long after she was confidently trained, a small scrap of torn newspaper fell to the floor. Happy spied it, walked over and wet it, expecting to be called a good girl and petted. Instead Mother flew into a rage and never trusted the poor dog again.

So when Mrs. Altschuler claimed that she found a hole in a Canadian blanket airing on her first-floor clothesline, Mother let her accuse the dog who was on a rope too short to reach it. Mother's criterion (one of her favorite words) for all behavior was, "What will the neighbors think?" and Happy was already in her bad graces. From then on when we children weren't home, Happy was relegated to our uninsulated upstairs back porch, whose floor was now covered with newspaper. She was more imprisoned than our Long Lane parolees or me. In the confined space she almost had room only to chase her own tail in circles, and I believe that slowly drove her crazy. Mother branded her "wild" and convinced Daddy that she must be gotten rid of. An ad to sell her was placed in the very newspaper Happy had trained on. While the ad ran, I suffered the twin agonies of heartbreak and a dire case of measles. The doctor warned that because there was no room on my body for any more red bumps, a second case of the disease was lurking beneath my skin waiting to break out. The adults decided that my eyes couldn't tolerate light, and the Venetian blinds in my bedroom were kept drawn, even when the maid spooned chicken soup into my mouth. To make things worse, Mother accidentally bought the wrong lotion to apply to the measles, and it made them itch far worse than before. They almost drove *me* crazy.

To cheer me up, I was moved from my dark bedroom to the living room sofa while the cruel lotion was replaced with the right stuff. But instead of being cheered, I was tormented as strangers came up the front stairs and passed by my couch to view my beloved Happy, displayed for sale in the kitchen. My only consolation was the thought that she would surely have a much better home with her next owner.

Happily, Happy wasn't sold. I was overjoyed when Daddy *gave* her to the man who sent coal down the chute into our basement for Mother to shovel into the furnace. The coal man had fallen in love with our dog and took her home to be loved by his children and wife as well. There she could live up to her name.

SCOUTING MIAMI BEACH

Mother's brother, Lou Libman, now owns a dress shop in Willimantic, but as a young man he helped out in their father's Hotel Savoy. In the winter of 1940–41 Lou hears about the success of new hotels opening up in Miami Beach, Florida, and decides to check out what opportunities may lie there. When school break starts, he leaves Aunt Dora to tend to both the store and their two older boys. He crams her ample but active mother (Granny Goodman) and their youngest kids (June and Ernie) into his old Studebaker with my mother, Roan, and me and heads south. My father was never a hotel man, and after the bankruptcy of his dress shops in the Depression, he's doing too well selling insurance to consider a new business risk. Uncle Lou has invited us along just for a vacation, and Daddy will follow later when his work slows down.

The first day of our trip, my uncle stops at a cousin's I never knew we had in Trenton, New Jersey, who generously finds room in her house to put us all up overnight. The next night after traveling south, we stop at a tourist home. Mother and Roan take the double bed in our room, and because I'm the smallest, Mother requests that a cot be set up for me. The owner regrets that he has no cot but offers a large crib and a full-size blanket. And that's how I, soon after my ninth birthday, try to sleep folded in half in a space designed at most for a toddler, dolefully looking out through the safety bars. I thank my lucky stars to have better accommodations the rest of the way to Miami Beach, where we all stay in a large, comfortable apartment in a residential area.

My cousin June is only a year older than I, and we've always been fast friends. Almost as soon as we unpack, she, Roan, and I become a secret club that meets on the enclosed back stairs of the apartment. We invite four-year-old Ernie to be a guest speaker, even though his diction still needs improvement. Standing on the landing facing us as we sit on the steps, he begins his first address with the words, "Ladies, I fink..." and proceeds to lecture about the thoughts that have taken up residence in his young mind. We three ladies exchange broad smiles and from this day on through old age, Roan and I may express opinions to each other by starting, "Lady, I fink..."

One day while Roan is reading, June and I take a walk in the neighborhood. All the modest houses we pass are pretty, but we're especially attracted by one with a whole corner made of opaque glass blocks. We've never seen such a thing before, and our admiration is so great that it must be expressed. Without a second thought, we turn off the public sidewalk. We stride right up to the front door. We ring the bell! The door opens, and an attractive middle-aged woman appears.

"We were just walking by, and we want to tell you how pretty we think your house is," we chime without hesitation. "We've never seen one partly made of glass before." The woman breaks into a big smile.

"Well, how nice of you! Would you like to see how it looks from the inside?"

We honestly were not angling for an invitation, and our surprised delight knows no bounds. Without a thought of caution, we enter. Paula leads us to the bathroom where the solid glass blocks form a corner. After we *ooh* and *ah*, she shows us the rest of the beautifully decorated house and introduces us to her sister Marianne.

"Let's have some milk and cookies," Paula invites, and the four of us sit around the kitchen table while the sisters ask us about ourselves and how we happen to be in Miami Beach. "Marianne and I are dancers, retired from the stage," Paula confides. "Shall we dance for you?"

We would love it! But we've already been out longer than we planned, and we tell the ladies that we're afraid our parents will worry if we don't get back to the apartment.

"Well, we enjoyed your visit. Please come back soon!" Marianne invites.

"May I bring my sister?" I ask.

"We would be very happy to meet her," Paula assures me.

Although Roan declines to join us at the home of strangers, a few days later June and I return to the glass-cornered house. Our new friends greet us with a big welcome and serve up cake and milk in the kitchen. This time our parents know where we are, and we can relax and stay longer. Paula rolls back the living room rug, puts a record on their turntable, and the two sisters perform dance routines that remind us of Ginger Rogers. It's better than in the movies! We clap our hands and gush and marvel at our good luck in meeting these surprising women.

After a while my father joins us in Miami Beach, with Little Aunt Rose in tow. Our family gets so busy sightseeing, picking oranges and kumquats off the trees, and lolling on the beach that June and I only have time for one more visit with Paula and Marianne. We say goodbye and thank them for their kindness to a pair of upstart children who suddenly appeared at their door. Then because Daddy must return to work, Roan and I to school, and Mother to her activities, we head home to Hartford, leaving Aunt Rose to return with her brother.

In time not only does Uncle Lou contract to manage the Ritz Carlton Hotel right on the ocean, but his brother,

Uncle Abe, is hired to manage the Betsy Ross Hotel further up the beach. They sell Lou's Willimantic dress shop and Abe's New Haven uniform store and move their families to balmy Florida.

I continue to shiver in the snow and sleet of New England winters with only a fond memory of two dancing sisters to warm me.

Transitions

WAR!

My uncles' move to Florida didn't happen right away, and on a December Sunday a year after our scouting trip, we were visiting Uncle Lou's family in Willimantic. As usual, after Granny Goodman had filled all the family bellies with a bountiful feast, Roan and I played on the Victorian wraparound porch with June, Ernie, and older brother Alan before we five took off for the neighborhood movie theater.

There was no need for a chaperone or a movie rating because the streets were safe, and no film included anything parents wouldn't want their child to see or hear. The matinee that day was a Five Little Peppers film. I identified with Phronsie, the youngest girl in the family.

After cavorting around on our walk home, we happily tumbled back into the house. But our frivolity skidded to an immediate stop when we saw everyone there in a state of shock. What could have happened? One of the adults somberly explained, "The Japanese have bombed Pearl Harbor, and now America will enter the War."

Although I was too young to grasp its full significance, I knew the news was alarming. I got my first taste of reality on the drive back to Hartford that night when we encountered one camouflaged truck after another, full of uniformed men, headed in both directions. I was bemused by such swift mobilization within hours of the attack. How did all these soldiers know where to go so soon? My ten-year-old mind could only figure that they must have known war was coming and been on the ready.

World War II directly affected our aunt and uncle's four oldest children. The first-born daughter was bizarrely widowed when an infection following botched dental surgery killed her husband on a stateside Army base. The second daughter became an Army nurse and married a fine doctor she worked with in the service. Cousin Murray played trumpet and was recruited as a bugler. Younger brother Alan also gave up some of his boyhood to serve in the Army. Luckily, all came home safely, and oldest Cousin Irma remarried after moving to Florida with the family.

The rest of us contributed what we could to the war effort. My parents, who habitually stocked canned goods in the basement in a common post-Depression reaction, now learned to shop more sparingly with ration books. A white A on a square black decal affixed to our car windshield announced that we could use very little gasoline for pleasure outings and family visits. Roan and I were always nervous that our car would be stopped by rationing police.

My fearful mother turned into an air raid warden. When sirens announced mock air raids and the rest of us hunkered down indoors, Mother patrolled the streets to make sure all blackout curtains had been drawn and to counsel any residents who were leaking light. I was so proud of her! And she sure looked smart in her grey Red Cross uniform with the round, red-bordered arm badge.

Because we were city people, I never would have dreamed that Mother, with Daddy on shovel, would transfer her indoor plant-growing talents so successfully to the Victory Garden that soon took over half of our back yard. Carrots! Swiss chard! Beets! Chives! The hollyhocks that climbed up the back of our house even shared their bed with prolific radishes. My folks both fell in love with city farming, though the neat rows of vegetables were returned to grass when the war ended.

Roan, now in high school, became a member of the Girls Auxiliary Messengers, preparing to carry communications from one air raid shelter to another. She also learned shelter survival skills. One of these was a game to keep one's mind off the fear of bombs falling, whose name I never learned. A paper-and-pencil word game, my husband and I play it to this day in time-killing situations that inhibit conversation. When folks around us notice, they ask what we're playing, and we teach them what we simply call The Bomb Shelter Game.

When Mother "flew up" with my Brownie troop and became our Girl Scout leader, she introduced many war-related activities into our troop agenda. We practiced sewing by hand-hemming diapers for refugee babies, and we knitted squares to combine for warm afghans. We rolled bandages for injured soldiers, and we all bussed to a downtown office to become a collating team for a thick new government manual. For many of us, the rewarding feeling of being a useful part of things laid the foundation for adult volunteering.

Roan and I each diligently saved money for U.S. Savings Stamps. When we had eighteen dollars and seventy-five cents worth of stamps pasted into a book, we could turn it in for a war bond that would pay twenty-five dollars after the war. One summer at Stannard Beach we gathered a small group of friends to write and perform a play—Cinderella—in the back yard of our rented cottage. A sheet on the clothesline was our curtain, the grass our stage, and borrowed chairs accommodated our audience. We scheduled the play when all the fathers would be down to spend the weekend with their families. Not only our parents, their friends and ours, but permanent residents up and down the beach paid ten cents apiece to watch the performance. Roan and I both bought Savings Stamps with our share of the gate.

Back on Blue Hills Avenue, word spread among the prolific Japanese beetle community that the Zaccagnino grapevines offered gourmet fare, and the leaves were besieged by the disgusting iridescent orange/green insects munching them into lace. The beetles clung to the leaves with sticky feet, but when we returned to Hartford, Roan and I pulled each one off with a little tug and dropped it into a glass bottle we carried. For this chore the Zaccagninos paid us by the bottle, and we also converted that money into Savings Stamps.

Tin was needed for the war effort, and every family stomped on its empty food cans to flatten them for collection. Smokers stripped the foil lining off the insides of their cigarette packages, and we kids rolled it into balls, adding any foil we harvested from gum wrappers and discarded cigarette packs we found in the gutter. We competed to see who could roll the biggest ball. How could we foresee that as adults, in an attempt to defend the environment, we'd be dumping aluminum cans, foil, and other recyclables into a barrel that mechanical arms empty into a city truck right in front of our own house?

It was not all fun and games. World War II reached out its cruel, dark shadow to grab even an impressionable young girl in the safety of America. I was disturbed that my parents kept their ears glued to what seemed like hourly radio newscasts whether at home or in the car. I kept hearing the word Nazis. I asked Roan, "Why are they listening to the same thing over and over? That's the same news we heard an hour ago." With repeated hearing, I was internalizing the unimaginable horror we heard unfolding. Initially we suspected, then we knew that Jews were being at first debased in their home communities, then deported to extermination camps where they were gruesomely tortured, experimented upon, and gassed to death just for being Jewish. At war's end the full extent of the animal savagery was revealed, and although my family had no relatives left in Europe and was safe in our Transatlantic democracy, the specter never leaves this American child of being sadistically targeted anywhere in the world for being born, through no choice of my own, into an unwanted people.

A PAIR OF STOCKINGS

My greatest personal sacrifice for the war effort was unintended. At the age of twelve, my cruller cousin David was going to escort me to a Young People's League dance in the vestry of Emanuel Synagogue. I had a new dress, golden moire hair ribbons, and my first grown-up pair of lisle stockings to wear in my new patent–leather, teen-heeled shoes. It wasn't a formal date, and since David and I had been playmates from early childhood, I wasn't nervous. But I was excited.

A couple of hours before I needed to get dressed for the dance, my mother called from Uncle Larry's house, where she and Daddy were visiting. Though "Loose Lips Sink Ships," as ubiquitous posters proclaimed, Uncle Larry and Aunt Sarah's son Melvin had just phoned from his Army post at Fort Devens and dropped their personal code word into an innocent chat to alert his parents that he was being shipped overseas the next day. Larry and Sarah were about to speed off to Massachusetts to embrace their son for what could be the last time, and my folks, who adored Melvin, were going along. Mother wouldn't be home to help me dress and send me off to the dance. I was deflated. I was affronted to think that my parents' nephew was more important to them than their own daughter until I realized that going to war was a bit more serious than going to a dance. Happily, my petulance faded before it could spoil my evening.

Besides, my sister was there to help me. Roan, who had started dating, shared my excitement about my first escorted party. She offered great support and helped me with my ribbons, but when it came time to put on the new stockings, they were not where Mother had told us! Frantic, I ransacked every drawer in our bedroom and then my parents', but I found no stockings. Since the adults were already en route, there was no way to contact Mother. My evening—my life!—was about to be ruined. But thank heavens for big sisters! Roan calmed me down and loaned me a pair of her own stockings. The crisis over, in spite of Mother's leaving me in the lurch, I fully enjoyed the dance.

The next day we learned that because Roan and I had brand new bedroom furniture, we weren't yet aware of a shallow drawer hidden behind an embellishment in the highboy. There Mother pointed out my waiting stockings. We had just not understood her directions.

Soon all of us were relieved to learn that Cousin Melvin had been assigned to a military dental clinic in London rather than the front line. But he still faced mortal danger from the Blitzkrieg. Every week I wrote to him at his APO address, giving a detailed synopsis of a movie I'd seen on the weekend. For the rest of his life whenever I was present, he'd tell anyone who'd listen how he had looked forward to his kid cousin's reviews. But his greatest distraction was waiting for him at the USO, where English girls volunteered to dance with lonely American soldiers. At war's end we all welcomed his vivacious Joyce when she arrived in America on a ship full of British war brides.

By then, with Air Force parachutes no longer demanding all of the new material, ladies were lining up around the block at Hartford stores to buy nylon stockings.

MY BAS MITZVAH

Emanuel Synagogue religious school taught Jewish ethics, history, and tradition to children on Sunday morning until they were old enough to join in adult services after class on Saturday. Young Roan and I weren't pondering religion as we walked to Sunday school each week. We were miffed that we couldn't be home when the newspaper came. We couldn't wait to spread the full sheets of colored funnies on the living room floor, lie on our stomachs in front of them, read about the adventures of Dick Tracy, and laugh to see a shirt button pop off the rotund belly of Smilin' Jack's friend Fatstuff into the open mouth of a waiting chicken. Forced to defer that pleasure till we got home, we complained vociferously.

One winter Sunday, the early morning cold demanded ski pants for the walk to the synagogue. By the time we headed home, it had so warmed up that I carried mine the whole mile slung across my bent forearm. When I finally dropped them on my bed and ran to share the funnies with Roan, my elbow, crooked under the pants' weight for so long, was too stiff and hurting to straighten out at once. My loud lamentation proved a strange catalyst for parental rethinking, and Roan and I were both allowed to drop the Sunday school classes in the spring.

I didn't know to be careful what I wished for. My sister was deemed far enough along in her religious education to end it altogether, but the folks weren't giving up on me. To replace the weekly discussion of morality and observance, they now enrolled me in private Hebrew language lessons with Mrs. Niemitz after school on Tuesday and Thursday. A bedroom of her second floor flat on Blue Hills Avenue had been converted into a classroom with a few rows of desks and chairs, where a half dozen of us bent to the task.

Although I didn't like giving up two afternoons for more school, I was surprised to find that without the funnies competing for attention, I easily learned to read the language, albeit slowly, and enjoyed it. I was proud that at Passover seders, when Dad and Grampa, eyes atwinkle at opposite ends of the extended table, raced each other through the Hebrew recitation of the tale of Exodus, I could occasionally locate in the *Haggadah* the very words they were reading aloud. Because I knew the story in English, it didn't matter that I couldn't translate a single word or kept losing my place.

When I was twelve, my language education was transferred to the makeshift classroom in Mr. Perkel's home-based Young Israel congregation. I was the only girl in the class, and by this time the boys were preparing for their Bar Mitzvahs. Instead of wasting more Hebrew lessons on a female, Mr. Perkel set me to reading Genesis in Yiddish, the language of the Diaspora. I did this by myself at a desk in the center of the room. All around me each boy was being taught to chant in Hebrew the prayers of the Sabbath service and his Haftorah accompaniment to the Torah portion read on the Sabbath of his Bar Mitzvah. My ears were constantly attuned to their instruction, and from continual repetition in the background, I couldn't help learning all the chanted blessings and six different Haftorahs. Sometimes I couldn't resist chanting along under my breath, and when my surprised teacher became aware of it, he began enlisting my help. On occasion when a boy stumbled on his words or sing-song chant, Mr. Perkel would direct, "Judy, show him how it goes." And I could.

In 1944 there was no tradition at the Emanuel Synagogue of girls becoming Bas Mitzvahs. Neither did the Emanuel have any stated prohibition against its daughters engaging in this rite of passage. As I sat week after week absorbing the boys' lessons, I began to dream of mastering my own Haftorah and proudly basking in the pride and honor of the ceremony on the pulpit...not to mention the joy of the ensuing celebration. Why not? I could do it! My dream hovered, inched forward, and became ever more fervent until it demanded to be confessed to my parents. I thought how proud they would be of me and how blessed they would feel to have nurtured a Daughter of the Torah! They had ensured that I had the needed education, and this would be a fulfilling culmination!

Excitedly, I presented my goal to Mother.

Her response: "It isn't being done."

I knew there was never any appeal from that kiss of death and let my dream fizzle.

The next year young Sylvia Sless became the first of many succeeding Bas Mitzvahs on the altar of the Emanuel Synagogue. Her mother didn't need precedent.

WHAT I LEARNED

When I was thirty-six years old, I proposed to my husband that we mirror a small wall in our West Hartford home. Unfamiliar with home décor, he asked, "Is that done?"

I assured him, "If I do it, then it will have been done."

THE LEPRECHAUN

Although Jones Junior High School was housed in a dreary building with mostly dreary faculty, Mary Finn was an enchanted leprechaun who led her students to golden knowledge at the end of our educational rainbow. She has remained an inspiration to me for a lifetime. Tiny, snub-nosed, never physically reaching the height of her teenage students, she soared over us in spirit and intellect.

Miss Finn whizzed through her day. The door from the corridor into her classroom was behind the forward-facing desks. Scurrying down the hall in Cuban-heeled oxfords, she would step one foot in the door after all the students were seated and slide—WHOOSH!—all the way to the front, her blonde curls bouncing. Homework papers would have been passed up the rows to the front desks, and she sailed across the front of the room collecting them. I don't know if anyone else ever chanced not having their homework done, but I sure didn't want to fail her well-stated expectations.

Aside from sharing the Latin language with us, Miss Finn's compelling picture of a living ancient Rome drew me back four times in later life to the rowdy modern city bursting with joy, history, and glorious art. Four times I stood transfixed among the majestic ruins of the Forum where Caesar stood and the marketplace of Trajan, with his ornately carved bragging column still intact. Forty years after eighth grade, I was tickled to still be able to translate the Latin commemoration of Roman conquests engraved on ancient arches and tablets.

Miss Finn taught English as well as Latin, and I was privileged to read A Tale of Two Cities in her class. Analyzing a book with her was like ferreting the very last bits of a luscious pecan out of its shell. She not only made the book come as alive as she had Roma Antigua, but she revealed and reveled in Dickens' writing tools. Occasionally she would ask one of us to teach the class while she sat among the students, and I was thrilled to be so chosen. Miss Finn was so inspiring that I even thought I had something to offer that day.

I'd wanted to be a writer since first grade, when The Hartford Times published my poem, Spectacles, written while temporarily wearing glasses. (The idea of singing came later.) In junior high I was on the school newspaper but no budding star. Mary Finn made me want to write something meaningful. I planned to dedicate it to her, but I have waited too long.

I AM NOT JOAN

The girl I played with most often was Joan Porter, daughter of my Brownie troop's assistant leader, Fan Porter. Fan was as fine a lady as my mother, the troop leader, but when none of us eight- and nine-year-old girls noticed Mother's arm up, her middle three fingers raised in the Girl Scout sign for silence, Mrs. Porter would place both her forefingers in her mouth, blow, and produce a whistle to rival a hurtling train. We loved her for it, and we'd shut up fast!

Joan's family lived on the second floor of a two-story house similar to ours, just a block away on Cornwall Street. They had an attic on the third floor like us, but nobody lived in theirs. The attic was only a little stuffy, and it housed as much interesting storage as Aunt Ethel and Uncle Frank's basement in Brooklyn. Most important was a trunk full of Mrs. Porter's cast-off clothes, high-heeled shoes and accessories, which we donned to strut around playing ladies.

Joan's mother, taller than mine, blonde, and severe-looking, came across as cool and sensible rather than warm and fuzzy. Because she left us pretty much alone with our own imaginations, the attic became a private haven to be enjoyed for hours.

Their house stood atop a grassy bank that rose from the public sidewalk. In winter Joan and I rolled down the snow-covered bank in our ski suits and in warmer weather rolled down the grass coatless. Summer or winter, Mrs. Porter always appeared after a while with a tray of refreshments.

"Would you like a cookie and some lemonade?" she'd ask.

Taught never to impose on anyone, it was impossible to say I would. My response was always a shrug and "I don't care." Oh, but I did care! I wanted that luscious-looking cookie! Nice lady, she handed it to me anyway.

Then one day atop that grassy hill, Mrs. Porter said kindly, "You know, if you're offered something, it's okay to say you'd like it. Don't say I don't care—say Yes please or No thank you straight out." This reminded me that at the moment when my Aunt Sarah offered me food or a gift, she'd always coach me, "Don't look at your mother" for approval. I also remembered that not long ago Fan Porter had taught me not to belittle myself in answer to a compliment, but to accept it and say a simple thank you. All at once an explosion of beautiful fireworks went off in my mind and my spirit, heralding a new notion: *I am worthy to receive what I am offered!* My self-esteem inched forward a notch and life seemed to open up a little. I wished it could have been my own mother who'd imparted such a valuable lesson.

I rarely invited Joan to my house after school. I had an attic, but someone was living in it. I had a basement, but in addition to three families' storage, it housed my father's workshop, the furnace, and the coal pile. The only play space our flat offered was the room where the maid slept or, in season, one of the outdoor porches. My mother didn't save her old clothes, shoes, and accessories for me, and I didn't have a lot of games like Joan's Parcheesi. Since our bedrooms and living room always had to be meticulous, and since the kitchen wasn't very private, why would anyone want to come to my house? I was always more comfortable visiting somewhere else.

Even my parents' own friends played second fiddle to the perfection of the house. Perhaps it was because my folks had lost so much in the Depression that Mother was driven to preserve what was left, but I knew little of that. At some point, she decided that the two ends of the maroon sofa were wearing down faster than the middle. "Everyone wants to sit next to the arms," she accused. Unable to protect both extremities at once, she nevertheless devised a scheme to deflect her guests from one end at a time. She rotated the rectangular polished wood coffee table from its centered position in front of the sofa to set it at a right angle to the right-hand cushion, blocking access to that side. In her zeal to protect those upholstered corners, I wondered, did she not care how weirdly unbalanced that looked? I almost howled with glee when a visiting lady friend, faced with the asymmetrical arrangement, wordlessly centered the table in front of the sofa again and plopped herself down (oh, excuse me, gently lowered herself) next to the forbidden arm. When she left, Mother did not move the table again, but I certainly wasn't eager to invite a friend home and be nervous about where she sat.

It seemed like Joan had a birthday party every year, and I met fun kids there who weren't even in our school. There were colorful decorations and balloons and interesting games to play for prizes. I only remember my parents making me one real birthday party and how grateful I was for it. Daddy delivered a memorable surprise when he kicked aside a small rug between the living room and dining room and performed a soft-shoe routine on the wooden threshold for my guests! It was the only time I ever saw him dance for an audience.

My twelfth birthday was memorable without a party. My sister handed me a beautifully wrapped box, and in it I found two tickets to the upcoming Ballet Russe performance of The Labyrinth. On the appointed evening, Roan took me on the bus to that performance—my first ballet! Oh, the excitement of the evening! Just the two of us—how grown up! The beauty of Bushnell Memorial Hall! The magic of the dancing! I became an instant balletomane. What an incredible gift!

Instead of being celebrated with a joyous Bas Mitzvah, my thirteenth birthday—only the second I remember sharing with classmates—was a disaster. The date coincided with Simchas Torah, a Jewish holiday I didn't remember hearing of before then. But that year Mother had a flash of inspiration: after the birthday meal, instead of playing games, my guests and I must walk to the synagogue and join the march up and down the sanctuary aisles to mark a new cycle of Torah reading from the Beginning. At the age of thirteen, we were patently too old to be marching with the younger kids. I was suffused with embarrassment and guilt to subject my invited guests to this activity, and I was forlorn to be denied my turn for party gaiety at home. After we walked back to the house, Mother just served cake before everyone was taken home. Not only did I not have a Bas Mitzvah, not only did I not have a birthday party, but now I felt like the biggest jerk in Jones Junior High.

Joan Porter got top grades in school. Mine were only a pinch lower, but when report cards came out, Mother challenged me, "Why aren't you like Joan?" I thought *Maybe if you were more like Joan's mother, I'd be more like Joan. But you are you, so like it or not, I am me.*

After the war, Joan's father, a building contractor, constructed a lovely single home for his family in West Hartford with the impressive innovation of a bathroom on each of the two floors! No longer living just around the corner, I rarely saw Joan outside of school after that.

At our high school graduation, she was one of two salutatorians whose academic records were tied. I'd guess Fan never questioned her why she wasn't valedictorian. I was grateful that my folks didn't give me any trouble about just being one of the speakers, delivering a humorous piece to lighten the proceedings. Joan went on to graduate from Smith College, marry a doctor, move out of state, and have several babies. I never saw her again.

I never did become like Joan.

A FAN IS BORN

One day when I'm fourteen, Mother is hosting her Mah Jongg game and has invited a woman I've never met to substitute for an ailing regular player. Mrs. Wetstone lives in another part of town, and when the afternoon is over, her son Howard comes to pick her up. While waiting for the last game to end, he spies my beautiful seventeen-year-old sister, and BAM, he's a goner! That very night he calls to ask for a date, and the pursuit begins which culminates in their marriage two years later.

Everyone knows that if a girl is ready when her date arrives, she looks too eager. When boys come to call for Roan, my job while she's stalling, fully ready, in the bedroom is to greet them, tell them she'll be out in a minute, and chat a bit with them during the wait. (If things start looking more serious, my folks will take over the job so they can size up the guy.)

Howard Wetstone makes my job easy. He asks me about school, how I like my teachers, whether I have a boyfriend, and if I like sports. When I answer the last two questions in the negative, he says, "If you want boys to be interested in you, you must be interested in what they're interested in." He gives me homework to complete by the next time he comes for Roan. He tells me the names of the eight baseball teams in each major league, and I must memorize them, with their correct league affiliation, and be able to recite them. This tickles my imagination, and I do it.

Roan has absolutely no interest in baseball, but while he's courting her, Howard teaches me the rudiments of the game, the names and positions of the players, the official terminology and nicknames in use, and a selection of shouts to cheer the team on. I love it all! In the summer when he comes to the beach for the day, he sneaks off into his car for a while, inviting me to join him in listening to the Red Sox game on the car radio. When Ted Williams gets up to bat, I love to hear Howard yell, "Bang a bingo, Ted!" I pick up the lingo, though with my ladyship training, I'll never yell it anywhere but in the front seat of that car or when I'm home alone. I listen to live and remote broadcasts of baseball on the radio whenever there's a game on, become familiar with the players on all the teams, and can recite the averages of the stars. I know the announcers, stats, and standings. Howard has given me an enormous gift that provides joy for a lifetime. And, incidentally, years later it does make me very interesting to one particular fellow.

MOTHER BREAKS HER PROMISE

The old black upright piano on which Roan has been learning to play classical music sits on the top landing of the stairs just outside our living room. At six years old I also come under her teacher's tutelage, but though I love the music, I don't want to practice and am easily allowed to drop the instruction. Several years later I have regrets and ask to take lessons again, only by now Roan has moved from classical to popular music and has a different teacher. Although I tell my folks I only want to learn classical, they refuse to deal with two teachers. So it's pop lessons with Mr. Lake or nothing.

I start unenthusiastically with him, but before the year's out, he sabotages my lessons anyway. Sitting on a chair next to my piano bench, he leans across me to point out something on the sheet music and braces his nearest hand on my thigh. Oh, oh, I've heard about things like this. Silently, with my eyes never leaving the music, I drop a hand from the keyboard and crack my bent elbow into his forearm FORTISSIMO. He quickly withdraws his hand. After he leaves, I tell my parents. Roan reports a similar experience, and our lessons end.

When I'm eleven, my folks come at me to choose another instrument to learn. Without hesitation I gleefully cry, "Drums!" Although I'm a girl and destined to remain short, I dream of banging the big bass drum in festive parades. On the other hand, I'd also love to play the rich-sounding tympani in the symphony. Or I might become another Gene Krupa on snares and cymbals!

Mother vetoes any drums because they aren't ladylike. Instead she chooses for me her favorite instrument, the cello. WHAT? In 1942, girls wear slacks only for play and don't own long dresses. As I sit in the school orchestra and place that damn cello between my open knees, my skirt rides up and reveals my stocking tops and garters. That's ladylike? I only want a hole to crawl into!

Furthermore, it hurts. Someday I'll see young kids with graduated-size instruments, but the beat-up cello the folks have rented for me now is a full-sized son-of-a-gun that overpowers me. It has also come without a cover. So I start schlepping this monstrous hunk of bare wood and strings over my hip down the hill from our home to my school and back up again later. Luckily, before long my cruller cousin rescues me. On orchestra days, David meets me at the top of the Holcomb Street hill and relieves me of the cello, while I carry his nicely dismantled trombone in its compact case.

But HELP! I'm being crucified by a nail! The one that protrudes from the bottom of my instrument won't anchor it on the floor as it's supposed to but keeps sliding forward, taking the cello with it. Daddy makes me a wooden block with a hole in it where the nail should anchor itself. Now the block *and* the cello slide away from me! With my thumb behind its scrolled neck, I have to keep pulling the musical monster back into position, and I suffer with a chronic aching thumb.

In the first year all of my instruction was in the elementary school music program. Now that I've gone on to junior high, my folks have arranged for a private teacher at the Julius Hartt School of Music. To get to lessons I have to heave the naked cello onto my hip, stand with it on the crowded bus going downtown, debark at the Aisle of Safety, and wait for the bus headed crosstown to Broad Street.

Picture standing in wet falling snow, joined at the hip to an outsized instrument, dreaming of the unprotected wood cracking, the pegs swelling, the strings slipping, the bridge collapsing, and the whole cursed thing finally dying of exposure!

My new teacher has an Italian name but speaks with a thick Russian accent. He has fearsome black, bushy eyebrows that put John L. Lewis to shame. Though he's intimidating, I'm not afraid of him; I just *intensely dislike* him.

For months Mr. Balastro has been harassing me to cut my nails for better placement of my fingers on the strings. Listen, my sister is slim and pretty, with long, wavy blonde hair, while I'm a chubby redhead. Roan gracefully glides; I bustle. But she chews her fingernails practically to the knuckle, while I get compliments on the nails I keep long, shaped, and polished. No way am I getting rid of those!

Finally in utter frustration, Mr. Balastro orders, "You cot yourrr fingerrrnails orrr you don't play cello!"

I say, "Fine, I won't play cello," sling my albatross on my hip, and take the next crosstown bus out of there.

Given the magnitude of my misery, my parents give in. But they are disappointed; now in spite of Roan's teaching me to love her seventy-eight-rpm symphonic records, I'm a kid without musical culture.

But wait! People begin remarking on my singing voice, and I'm accepted into the junior high choir. Although I've only attained the age of thirteen, folks are suggesting that I take voice lessons. My parents have been three times burned with my piano and cello failures, and voice lessons aren't even recommended till the age of sixteen, but Mother says okay, I can start lessons when I reach that age.

"Promise?" I ask.

"Promise," she agrees.

Three years go by, and now I'm in the Weaver High School chorus, Weaver glee club, Inter High choir, All State choir, and have been tapped for the All New England Music Festival in Vermont. It seems that if I have any talent, it's not in my fingers but in my vocal chords. Yet my mother is stalling about lessons. I sing a solo at a Weaver concert and the Inter High director, who's on staff at the Hartt School, approaches my parents in the auditorium.

"It's a terrible waste if your daughter doesn't study voice," Elmer Hintz says. "You ought to have her audition at Hartt."

"Thank you, we will," Dad says, as if I haven't been begging for permission. And so finally I'm back on the bus to Broad Street, but this time happy.

For placement, I sing for the head of the voice department. Her eyes light up, her body electrifies, and she gleefully proclaims, "I will teach you myself!" On the crosstown and uptown buses home, I'm ecstatic!

I burst into the house and tell Mother, "Helen Hubbard will teach me herself!"

Mother looks at me coolly and says, "Now call her and tell her you won't be taking lessons."

I admit that as a teen, I am not a stranger to hysterics. "Why?" I plead. "Why, why, why?" I can think of nothing I need to be punished for. I know that my folks have spent years climbing back from the Depression, and I cry, "Is it the money?" I could accept that. But Mother denies it, and no other reason is forthcoming. Then I remember that when times were worse there was always money for piano and cello lessons. I do not understand.

I remind her, YOU'RE BREAKING A PROMISE, the greatest sin in my personal code. She's not impressed. When Dad comes home he admonishes me not to be disrespectful to my mother, but he won't give me an answer either. What can I do but tearfully call the Hartt School to cancel lessons?

My friends in every choir share my outrage and despair. Alex in Inter High tells my story to his private voice teacher, and she wants to see me. I'm enchanted with Rhea's studio; it has strings of colored beads for a door, exotic trappings, and she herself is dressed like a gypsy. I know her reputation as a fine teacher, and when I sing "Ave Maria" for her, she says I have talent.

"Do you have any money?" she asks.

"I get two dollars a week for lunch money. I don't need to eat lunch, but I do need bus fare." (I'm saving the wages from my part-time job for college expenses.)

"I will teach you for one dollar a week," Rhea says, and we start conspiring how to keep it secret. Should she ever have to call my house to cancel a lesson, she will leave a coded message, identifying herself as a fictional friend. If needed, I will identify assigned lessons as choir music.

I study happily with Rhea for almost a year, until I solo at another Weaver concert. Again Mr. Hintz insists to my parents that I should be at Hartt. Only this time he does something about it—I am offered a scholarship. Parents relent, Rhea wishes me well, and I start eating lunch again. Helen Hubbard's schedule is now full, but she refers me to a respected young teacher who specializes in coloratura sopranos. Peggy takes me to seminars to demonstrate how she teaches, and we both receive valuable feedback.

I'm now applying to colleges, and the New England Conservatory of Music offers me an automatic one-hundred-dollar scholarship without an audition. I'm also accepted into the liberal arts program at the University of Connecticut.

I've been singing with the Connecticut Opera Association, which provides the chorus for professional operas staged in town, and I'm on stage with two stars from the Met who've come to Hartford to perform. In Cavelleria Rusticana, I sing a one-note duet with Regina Resnick because no other soprano can reach the high note, and I am so full of myself! In I Pagliacci, I'm thrilled when Ramon Vinay, as the tragic clown, actually touches me—pushing me aside in a stage gesture while he sings of his anguish.

But after curtain calls I look at Vinay and think, *In this piercingly cold weather, he's taken the train from New York to Hartford, being careful to protect his throat. Tonight he'll sleep in the Bond Hotel, which is getting pretty shabby. Tomorrow he'll take the train back to New York, and who knows when and where he'll be offered another role?* The up-in-the-airness jolts me. I do not want to live a life without an anchor. I go home and tell my parents that I will decline the New England scholarship and enroll in UConn.

After such a fuss and furor, when I graduate high school, my musical education is over. I sing in choirs and productions when there's room in my life, but I don't continue lessons or vocalize in the intervals between them. By the time I'm accepted into the Phoenix Masterworks Chorale twenty-five years later, my range has sunk from coloratura almost to tenor.

Roan does not ever play piano, I don't play cello, and the years have had their way with my fingernails. When my own children are nearly grown, I once again ask my mother why she broke her promise about voice lessons.

This time she answers. "I wanted to teach you not to set your heart on things so fervently."

I tell her about Rhea and that what I learned is that if my heart is set on something, I can find a way to do it.

Even though I may not want it forever.

THE LIBRARY

Imagination, the great escape hatch, was easily found in the books on the shelves of the Hartford Public Library. Once I outgrew Mother's Wednesday night ritual of bringing home a batch of books, I selected my own at the Northwest Branch, housed in an unadorned storefront on Albany Avenue. Before choosing new reads, I'd review those I'd just finished for the encouraging librarian, and she'd enter the titles onto a list which earned me a reward after the tenth one. But when I recapped my favorite, The Great Geppy—the tale of a talking red-and-white-striped circus horse—the librarian's demonstrated delight was all the reward I needed.

At the end of the school year, patrons could take out an unlimited number of books for the whole summer. Reading them at the beach was as delicious as a mint hot fudge sundae. They even rivaled the large stock of movie magazines Roan and I discovered in the cottage we rented each year before our folks bought their own. Once I reached puberty, on the days my new monthly visitor prevented me from swimming, I was happy to spend all afternoon immersed in a book on our screened porch.

In the library, one tool had always intrigued me. To check out books, the librarian used a pencil with a small rubber date stamp clamped to the shaft. She stamped the due date on a card taken from a pocket inside the book's cover and wrote the patron's library card number next to it by merely tipping the pencil. I wanted to do that!

Then imagine the thrill when in August 1947 I was offered a paying job as a "page"! I only had to promise to produce my working papers as soon as I became sixteen in October. Surrounded by books, I could help people use the library, and I got to wield the fun pencil-stamp when relieving at the Circulation desk.

There were other perks. After Forever Amber shocked (and titillated) the world, any work considered racy was represented by a bright blue wooden facsimile of it on the public shelf. A patron had to bring the wooden replica to Circulation, show an adult library card, and ask for the real thing. I'd then procure the actual book from the back room, and this was the way we kept inappropriate volumes out of the hands of young people. Although only a small number of adults had the courage to ask for God's Little Acre, I managed to read the whole thing during breaks in the back room. I found books about girls who entered various careers more interesting.

In addition to checking books out and in, repairing and shelving them, helping patrons find particular volumes, filing Due Date cards, and maintaining the card catalogue, I started a story hour on Saturday mornings. It was such fun to read picture books and fairy tales to the children, using different voices for the various characters! After singing the role of the left-behind lame boy in Weaver High's performance of The Pied Piper operetta, I told my library kids the story, singing all the parts. They ate it up, and from then on no matter what story I read or told, I put most of the dialogue into song and got the children to join in. It was the city's only musical story hour, and I don't know if the kids or I had more fun!

I was thus happily employed, but not fruitfully enough to build up much of a fund for the college extras I'd need in another year and a half. On Saturdays Mother helped out friends, the Swayes, in their S&A variety store on Park

Street as a super saleslady. Occasionally Dad volunteered his old dress shop skill to decorate their show windows. One spring weekend I took leave from the library to help make up Easter baskets in the attic of the S&A. It was fun, and the pay was good. When I was invited to be a Saturday sales clerk on the main floor, I couldn't afford to turn down the higher wage. I hated to leave my library patrons, especially the children, but I could enjoy serving a different kind of customer. I ruefully gave my notice to the Northwest Branch, not knowing that my love affair with libraries would lead me to become a board member of one and a long-term volunteer at another in my adult life.

NOW I AM ONE

I'm so happy for Roan that she's going to be married, but it doesn't really hit home until I see it in print. Today a mild affliction has kept me in bed and feeling punk. When *The Hartford Times* is delivered late in the afternoon, Mother opens it to the Society page and, beaming, hands it to me in my bed. There is a picture of my beautiful sister, and Mr. & Mrs. L. Daniel Horowitz are announcing the engagement of their daughter Roan to Howard Wetstone. I didn't know it was going to be in the paper, and I'm caught off guard. I do not beam; I have a sinking feeling. I find myself helplessly welling up, and quiet tears begin to spill over. I am going to lose my lifelong buddy, roommate, and teacher. I already feel lonesome for her.

Soon the engaged couple, their four parents, and I go out to dinner together. Howard has no siblings. Leaving the restaurant, we walk to our cars along a narrow sidewalk. Howard's parents are walking side by side. Next come Roan and Howard, side by side. They are followed by my parents, next to each other. I'm bringing up the rear by myself. I look at the couples in front of me and feel acutely alone. I wonder if I will ever have anyone to walk beside me. Roan looks back and must sense this, because she and Howard drop back and bracket me, even though there's not room for three on the sidewalk. Although it sweetly shows me that I won't be forgotten, it underlines that I have no one of my own. From now on, I am solo.

Roan and Howard are married in a private banquet room at the Algiers restaurant in Farmington. Roan looks chic in a smart grey suit with pink hat and gloves. At sixteen years old, wearing a simple navy blue dress, I am not only her maid of honor but will sing "Because" during the ceremony. Waiting for it to start, I get an attack of nerves and quietly confess to my father that my G.I. system is threatening mischief. Uncle Larry is standing nearby, and after conferring, the brothers take me out to the restaurant's bar and order me a blackberry brandy to settle my innards. I feel a bit naughty drinking it, but it tastes good and best of all, it does the trick! When the moment comes, I am able to lovingly offer up my song to my cherished sister.

MY FIRST DATE, OR

IT'S HELL BEING SHORT

I'd just been asked out by the most gorgeous boy in the class! Long had I sighed over his amazing brown eyes and long lashes, and I was thrilled to know that behind his quiet demeanor, he'd noticed me, too!

But Mother wouldn't allow me accept his invitation. "If I let you start dating at fourteen," she'd said, "You'll be blasé by the time you're sixteen." I had to tell Stuart that I couldn't go out with him yet, and he never asked me again.

Now Marty, a fellow choir member and school newspaper reporter, has invited me to a movie—not at the Lenox but downtown! At sixteen I'm finally old enough to accept my first formal date, and on the appointed day we take the bus to the Loew's Poli theater on Main Street. Mother has insisted that I wear a tall bright green hat knitted in the shape of a cylinder, and I feel like an idiot. But it fits close on the head and if I take it off once out of Mother's sight, my hair will be a mess.

After the movie Marty and I walk to an ice cream parlor, where I order a milkshake for the first time in my life. When it's delivered, I eye the thing in utter dismay. There it sits on the marble table in front of me in a tall glass with a straw sticking out of it—and the top of the straw is level with my eyes! If I bend it, the thick shake will clog at the bend and never reach my mouth. Must I kneel on my seat or stand above my confection to access the straw? What a spectacle that would be!

After a few agonizing moments of reflection, I pick up the glass in two hands and lower it almost to my lap. Now I can successfully suck up the shake. Whew, what a relief!

It's a life lesson. With the up and down of years, I level out at an even five feet. I learn to bring my car cushion into restaurants so that I don't have to reach up for my food or lower it to my lap. Thus do I triumph over the conspiracy of those who design restaurant booths with dropped seats and chest-high tables.

Incidentally, I don't believe I've ever been blasé about anything in my life. Whether at home or out, after fifty-six years of marriage I still feel a fillip of joy when I'm on a date with my husband.

But I don't like milkshakes.

STANNARD BEACH

MONDAY THROUGH FRIDAY

In summer, much of my parents' social circle leaves Hartford to string itself out along the shoreline road at Stannard Beach in Westbrook, Connecticut. At the beach there are some different Mah Jongg and Pinochle players, children of different ages from scattered schools become friends, and physical activity increases. Yet every year the basic flavor is familiar and comfortable.

The first Friday after school lets out in June, the husbands drive their wives and children an hour and a half to the seaside community. As soon as our family hits the town of Deep River, still twelve miles short of our destination, my father inhales luxuriously and exults, "Smell that salt air!"

"It's too soon, Daddy," Roan and I counter, "You can't smell it from here!"

"Yes, you can," he insists. "Stick your nose up in the air and breathe deeply."

We don't agree, but we humor him. "Oh, yeah, Daddy, the smell of the ocean."

While the folks go into the grocery to stock up on food for our cottage, Roan and I amuse ourselves in the car by singing the old spiritual over and over:

Dee-ee-eep River,
My home is ohhh-ver Jordan...

Down at the beach, the menfolk spend the weekend settling their families in, then drive back to Hartford alone on Sunday night. We gals live in an isolated matriarchal society during the week. There are no males of breadwinning age and no family cars. The next Friday evening the men reappear like trekking penguins returning to find their own families. This is repeated every weekend of the summer until the kids have to prepare to hit the books again the Wednesday after Labor Day.

I'm lucky there are girls around my age to be friends with. We toughen our soles walking barefoot along the hot asphalt road to visit each other or congregating on the scorching sand in front of someone's cottage. Then we cool our feet rehearsing a graceful water ballet to perform for our parents at the end of summer.

And what are girls without a secret club? Some families have sailboats or motorboats, but my folks' rowboat is perfect to take out into the shallow water over a sandbar and scuttle, lifting and resettling its overturned frame to form an air pocket between the water and its upended bottom. Then standing on the mudflat, our bodies submerged but heads in the air pocket, we conduct a secret meeting. We are tickled that anyone on the beach will see only an overturned boat and not guess we're there.

Westbrook is on the Connecticut side of Long Island Sound, and we bet in low tide that we can wade all the way across to the New York shore. But when we encounter water over our heads, we're forced to abandon our goal. We throw ourselves in and start executing our favorite strokes. Swimming home at high tide, we remember to skirt the submerged cluster of boulders near shore just waiting to scrape the stomachs of the unwary. As we wade into the beach, we step carefully to dodge sneaky crabs that love to take a startling nibble of bare toes.

After school starts in the fall, my family returns to the deserted beach just for the weekends. I get a rush of joy diving right into the middle of September's heavy, frothing breakers as they raise themselves high before crashing against the shore. Or I stand planted and wait for one to knock me over. Sputtering salt water and seaweed and laughing, I regain my feet to wait for the next big one. Maybe I'll dive in or jump it, or maybe I'll let it take me. The ocean is my playmate, and autumn is my favorite time to be there!

During the summer there's plenty of fun on land. I spend many days playing Monopoly, though I'm not too happy with those who claim that a little friendly cheating at the bank enhances the game. Often I play against purple people. I'm grateful that I never have to be slathered like them with gentian violet to treat impetigo.

We girls have watched our mothers play Mah Jongg for so many years that we know the game as well as they, and we feel like adults mixing and playing the tiles. We all confess to loving the distinctive sound they make clicking against each other as we move them around the table. On July 6, 1944—an idyllic day—we're playing Mah Jongg on a friend's oceanfront porch with the sea breeze riffling our long hair. Suddenly Fan Porter appears in our midst in obvious shock. She has come to relay unthinkable news. There's been a terrible fire at the Ringling Brothers circus in Hartford. Many people have died, been horribly burned, or been trampled in the stampede to escape. We are stunned into silence and leave the tiles untouched on our racks to join her at the radio for more details.

As the week progresses, we learn with heavy hearts of classmates who have died or lost family members. Someone's aunt comes to the beach as a respite from serving as a nurse at the overflow morgue in Hartford. While folks sit in a horseshoe before her, she vividly describes the gruesome and heartbreaking sights she's seen. I WISH I HAD NEVER HEARD HER.

But slowly life resumes at Stannard Beach.

Occasionally a husband or visitor temporarily leaves a car with one of the mothers who knows how to drive. My mother doesn't, and we only have one car, anyway. But those others allow us to get off the beach and into the nearby town of Saybrook. One day Mrs. Reuben announces that she's going to take her daughter Barbara and a group of us girls to a restaurant there and teach us how to properly eat a whole Maine lobster. It takes some technique to do justice to this scrumptious delicacy, and after paying a fortune, many people overlook a good portion of its celestial offerings.

As we're seated at the table, waiters tie cotton bibs around our necks. When a baked stuffed lobster—so superior to boiled!—is laid before each of us, our hostess shows us how to use the nutcracker to open the large red claws and switch to the special fork to dig the meat out of the claws and body. But then, although she commends us for being well-mannered ladies, she declares that when eating lobster there must be no holds barred! She shows us how to use our bare hands to tear the narrow feelers off the main shell, our teeth to bite the small amount of tasty meat from the juncture and our lips to suck more of the delicacy out of the feelers. It's girl vs. lobster, and we are not to let an ounce of the crustacean escape us! I consider this afternoon a crucial part of my education.

Another time someone's nephew shows up with a car and tells us to pile in; he's going to take us to the movie in Saybrook. A rare movie, breaking up the fatherless week, is a notable treat. And this is no ordinary vehicle. I finally get to ride in that fun space I've always wanted to try—a rumble seat! The nephew instructs me to put one foot on the flat circular step above the rear tire and hoist myself into the extra steel-enclosed upholstered space that folds down outside the back of the car. Another girl climbs in next to me, and we grin all the way into town with the wind blowing through our hair and no window between us and the scenery. Two other girls have a turn on the way back.

Before long we kids are offered another lift into Saybrook. There's a carnival set up in the lot next to the theater. In a few weeks we'll start shunning movie houses and anywhere that crowds gather, to avoid contracting dreaded polio. No one argues with that rule because we've all seen those awful newsreels of children trapped in iron lungs. I'm surprised that Mother even lets us go to the carnival now, because in any season they are wicked places where "there are all kinds of people" from whom her daughters must be sheltered. Perhaps about now she herself is feeling stir crazy on our behalf, and, chaperoned, we will only spend a short time at the carnival before we go next door to the small theater.

From the top of the Ferris wheel I look down on the adjacent roulette booth. I've never gambled before, but once on the ground, I place a dime on the counter over a number I pick randomly. The wheel spins and spins and—amazement! It stops on my number! My prize is placed into my arms: a stuffed doll the size of a plump live child in a seated position, covered in colorful chintz. Just then the movie is about to start and the car's too far away to take the doll there. I sling her over my shoulder and cajole the theater cashier not to charge me for the extra seat she'll occupy. He agrees, and my Lucy behaves well as she sits next to me during the film and comes home on my lap in the car.

Now, don't get the impression that there are no boys our age at the beach or in our thoughts. Those at hand are sometimes included in our Monopoly games and impromptu parties but never at Mah Jongg, as our fathers are not. We girls all have a mild crush on Ronnie, the most adorable guy at Stannard, but he has character and carries it well. Most of us have someone back in Hartford we think about, too. In sixth grade Jerry was the big heartthrob, and just before school ended, he let it be known that he'd made a secret list of the girls he liked. This raised much conjecture in the under-the-boat meetings at Stannard Beach, and the scuttlebutt coming out of Hartford was that Judy Horowitz was second on the list. Me? The unbelievable news gave my self-image another little nudge. I could always use one.

Although the whole female world is swooning over Frank Sinatra, I decline to be one of *that* mob. Instead I drop my nickel into the floor-standing jukebox at the Westbrook corner store to hear Dick Haymes sing, "The More I See You," and dream my romantic dreams.

THE ENTREPRENEUR

I don't spend all my hours playing at Stannard Beach; I'm also involved in two commercial ventures. I'm partners with Roan and her friend Harriet in a clamming business, and Harriet loans me her bicycle so that her kid brother and I can run a mail service. Neither Roan nor I have ever owned a bicycle, but classmates have taught me how to ride theirs.

Mail for seasonal and permanent beach residents is sent to General Delivery at the post office in Westbrook center. The town is a mile from the beach, where the ladies are without transportation. There are no sidewalks along the Boston Post Road, busily trafficked by interstate cars and heavy trucks. One summer the coed daughter of permanent beach residents is swiped and killed by a semi veering around a curve where she's sitting on a roadside fence waiting for a bus. It's stomach-turning and tragic to pass officials culling bits of her skin from the scene for days after the accident.

But Harriet's brother Arthur and I block such thoughts from our minds. We're thinking about service to our clients as we pedal bikes along the post road into town, where we have contracted with Stannard residents to pick up their mail and deliver it door to door back at the beach. It's a convenience for them and a profitable enterprise for us. As long as we stay well on the shoulder of the road, the ride is safe and pleasant.

Sometimes after collecting the mail at the post office, we bundle it and keep it with us while we go next door to Neidlinger's, the general store. Coming in from the bright sun, the spacious dark interior is soothing, and it smells good. The cordial owners come forth to chat with us, and there's an endless variety of sundries, trinkets, and snacks to explore before we head on back to complete our route.

My other business is at the end of the beach road, where two sandbars stretch toward a barnacled jetty. The first one my partners and I come to is a bare mudflat, and the next is totally covered with grey wave-worn rocks of medium size. At the second, one of us tosses a rock softly onto the bed. If there are steamer clams under that spot, they are startled by the percussion, stretch tiny strong-muscled protuberances out of their shells, and send up self-incriminating spritzes of water. If we're lucky, a host of these little fountains make known the presence of a good-sized population.

Now starts the race between man and mollusk. The clams realize they've been found out and start burrowing deeper into the mud under the rocks as one of us thrusts in our pitchfork and digs out a shallow hole. We all sit or squat and run our bare fingers along the hole's sides and bottom till we feel the two close, sharp edges of a double shell. We don't wear clamming gloves because we want to use the sensitivity in our fingers to discover our prize. Sometimes before a clam closes itself tight for protection, its edges will deliver a sharp, shallow cut. That's okay; we respect him as a worthy opponent and accept the minor wound as a price of doing business.

We pull many clams out of the sides of the hole and dig it deeper with our fingers as they burrow down in the smelly muck. When the last of the speedy fellows seem to have escaped us, we toss rocks in other directions and move to the most promising field of responding waterspouts.

The produce man who drives around the beach streets

selling fresh fruits and vegetables from within his truck has given us a generous supply of the pint and quart baskets he uses to measure out his offerings. Every evening we canvass the length and breadth of Stannard Beach to take orders for clams to be dug the next day when the ebb tide recedes from the sandbars. The clams are special-ordered by the pint or quart, and as we capture the sea's gift we fill up baskets for our customers. We drop any with broken shells, along with a bounty of perfect ones, into galvanized pails for our own families. Most people want the meaty large and medium sizes, but our favorite client is Mrs. Chidsey, a permanent resident who's lived here a long time before my parents' friends discovered it. Because she believes the smallest clams are the sweetest, we have no discards and gratefully fill her baskets.

My mother has kept kosher all her years, although she's conceded to having only one set of dishes at the shore instead of the separate ones she keeps for meat and dairy meals back in the city. Since only fish with scales are considered kosher, shellfish is verboten in the sacred diet. But coastal-dwelling heathens may succumb to the lure of the lobster and proclaim that his hard red shell is actually two big scales, making him permissible. Now Mother is seduced by the constant temptation to try her daughters' clams, and she falls in love at first taste. Many days when Roan and I come home with our pail full, we set it under the outdoor shower until as much incidental sand as possible sinks to the bottom. Mother boils an oversized pot of water, and we dump in our catch. The tightly closed bivalves open to the steam. Mother strains the water to remove any lingering sand and serves it as clam broth with crusty rolls and butter. We pull the clams themselves out of their parted shells by their thin protruding necks and rinse them in more broth. After pulling away its loose wrinkled black "scarf," the neck becomes a handy handle to dip the whole thing into a bowl of melted butter and drop it between waiting teeth.

We raise our eyes to the ceiling in ecstasy.

Now a corrupted seafood lover, Mother comes down to the clam flats to watch us work. Although it looks like it might be fun, there's no way this prim, formal lady is going to squat or sit in her dress and stockings on the rocky, mucky ground. But one Friday Dad brings her a surprise—a short-legged round wooden stool he's concocted in his basement workshop back in Hartford. The minute she sits on it in rare sport clothes and starts stalking clams, Mother is hooked. Low tide occurs in mid-afternoon that day. Before we know it, dinnertime has arrived, and no food is prepared. But we cannot pry Mrs. Horowitz away from the clam flats until the incoming tide starts licking at her feet. What fun!

Neither Roan nor Harriet joins me on the days when I move away to the smooth sandbar with a child's plastic pail and shovel. This real estate is inhabited by the most wonderful bright red, long, fuzzy, undulating worms beloved of salt water fish. I have a stock of them ready when Dad arrives, and we load them onto our boat with our other supplies and row out to deep water. Our drop lines are lengths of thick dark-green cord wound around squares of folded cardboard. After attaching hooks, sinkers, and bobbers, we thread the red wriggly worms onto the hooks and unwind the lengths of line overboard. If we're as lucky as usual, dinner tonight will consist of broth with rolls, steamed clams, coleslaw, and grilled cunners and flats. Blowfish, skates, and any small catch will have been thrown back.

Because Roan doesn't take much to worming and fishing, I most often enjoy the peaceful pastime with my father alone or with one of his amiable friends along. I'm proud when they commend me, even though a girl, for not chattering and scaring the fish away. On a little rowboat in the Atlantic Ocean I slip out of my entrepreneurial role and become just one happy daughter.

STANNARD BEACH WEEKEND

The whole place livens up once the husbands and fathers arrive on Friday night. Now there's muscle and a kind of vibrancy. The guys are taking a break from their weekday routines and are heartily enjoying themselves.

They reconnect with their wives, children, and each other. They swim and sunbathe, too macho to apply Coppertone lotion. They barbecue. They take each other's families to the movies in Saybrook, Clinton, Madison, or Essex. They play volleyball and softball and pitch horseshoes.

Before my folks buy their own place, we share a rental cottage with Aunt Rose, Uncle Harold, and Billy. Our large, darkly hirsute uncle is happy to go into deep water with Roan and me, submerge so that we can climb on his shoulders, then rise and let us dive off that high perch. He's fun!

Next to our cottage is an empty dried-grass lot outfitted with a volleyball net. The men often gather here to play. At first it amuses my father's cohorts to let a young girl play on their team for a while, but when my serves fall unreturned in enemy territory, I'm invited to become not only a regular but their permanent server. With the indulgence of the opposing team, my father's side rotates around me, leaving me always in the serving corner. I'm so proud!

Then one day after we've been playing for an hour or so, my mother walks by the volleyball game. She spots me and throws a fit, exclaiming, "Your lips are black! You've got sunstroke!" How could those awful men be so irresponsible as not to notice, she chastises. I don't feel a bit hot and protest loudly, but Mother drags me into the shade of the cottage, sits on the ground, and insists I lie down with my head in her lap until I cool off. In full sight of my teammates! Wham! In one fell swoop, The Spoiler reduces me from a superstar among men to a coddled baby. I don't know if I'm more furious with her or with my father for not demurring. I suffer absolutely no untoward physical effects from the sun and go back to playing with the guys the next day, but the easy camaraderie has been destroyed. Now my teammates keep a defensive watch on the child among them to make sure she isn't getting fried and Mamma doesn't come yelling.

Sometimes from a different corner of that weedy lot comes the robust clang of horseshoe against stake. What a glorious sound! Occasionally when the menfolk are gone, we kids try our luck with ringers and leaners, but we have to admit that we do better with thudding rubber quoits

For the fathers' good-natured softball games at a nearby schoolyard, my sister, a couple of girlfriends, and I are the cheerleaders. It takes several vehicles to transport everyone there, and the players take up so much room inside that we four gals scrunch ourselves into the trunk of one car. One lies horizontal as far back as she can squeeze and breathe, and the other three sit face out, knee-to-chest and hold the lid open as the driver slowly makes his way to the ball field. My father has always said, "Ten can ride comfortably in a Ford… if they're well acquainted."

As men do, the teammates assign each other nicknames. My father is Dapper Dan because he's a tidy man, well dressed even in sport clothes. Using those creative names, we girls produce programs to distribute to bystanders and devise chants to spur the players on. While we have no special costumes and don't do much dancing, we cheerleaders manage to have a whale of a lot of fun.

After many happy seasons at Stannard Beach, when sons and daughters become old enough to hold summer jobs and prepare for college, our families stop coming. New people move in, and a whole different community is ready for the next generation.

SO IF THE SUN IS SHINING, WHY IS IT RAINING?

MIXED UP

A few years down the line, the sunshiny times at Stannard are overtaken by a whirling storm gathering force within me. Sometimes at high tide it sends me to the inlet beyond the clam beds to commune with breakers crashing white on the rocks, sending up spumes of naked force to match my inner turbulence.

I am full of hatred. Not intense dislike—*hate*!

I hate that Mother is standing in my way—so intent on her image of what she wants me to be that she cannot see who I am. She is determined to mold me into a lady, an aristocrat, or at the very least, a doctor's wife. I want to become a person: me. But I need to find out who that is. I know that I'm voracious for life but have no intention of hurting myself. Yet just as Mother pulled me out of the volleyball game, she'd pull me out of life lest I play too energetically.

I chalk up no credit for her letting me ride a borrowed bike on the dangerous Boston Post Road or attend a carnival in polio season, nor for her serving up the non-kosher clams I dig. She is the oppressor.

I hate it that Mother is so ladylike that she sneezes with her mouth closed, "Ch," when I know what loud, unguarded words can spew forth when she's angry. Even proper Aunt Rose, raised by the same parents, corrects me, "Judith, we lahff *tee hee,* not HA HA." But God's gift of laughter is so generous that I don't want to disdain it any more than I want to endanger the precious eyesight He gave me by reading in poor light on Shabbos. I believe a hearty laugh makes God smile. I think a cruel word—in any language—makes Him frown. And I will not smother a sneeze demanding to be free. I am the wrong clay for sculpting an aristocrat.

In my unbearable rage against Mother, there's no one to turn to but the roaring ocean. Roan doesn't oppose her. Dad, a generally soft and loving man, is stern in his demand that I unfailingly "Respect your Mummy." I grit my teeth. I have never called her Mummy, and I ask him why she can't respect me. Though I regret that he's caught in our crossfire, I feel abandoned, without an ombudsman. There is no prince to rescue me.

At the same time I am in a great struggle with myself. I don't seem to belong anywhere. Why am I never accepted? I relive the hurt of all those years in the primary grade classrooms where girls who were unfriendly to me got overflowing basketsful of valentines while I received only a pitiful few—mostly from kids who sent a blanket delivery to everyone in the class. Why do schools sponsor that potential for pain? When a new copper-headed girl entered our sixth grade class, why did a group of girls suddenly tell me at recess, "There's only room for one redhead," run off with her and never play with me again?

In high school I'm not asked to join a sorority, but my friend Eudy is kind enough to invite me to sit with her when she eats lunch with her gang. Why is she included and I left behind? A pretty Sabbath school classmate tells me she's dating a different boy every Saturday night. Each year one different fellow takes me out regularly, but they're from Hartford High School across town, and nobody else is ringing my phone. *What's the matter with me?*

STOOD UP

West Hartford's Temple Beth Israel holds a prom in June, and of course, I'm not invited. Nancy, a sometime friend since first grade, fixes me up for the dance with her out-of-town cousin, Frankie Hammer. He's just a couple of years older but suave and handsome. I'm beguiled, and he shows that he's really interested in me. When we realize that I'll be at Stannard Beach while he's working his summer job at neighboring Bill Hahn's resort, he tells me to save July 4 and he'll come to pick me up for the fireworks. I hope he doesn't see that I'm already glowing.

I'm in a high state of anticipation when the holiday arrives. As the afternoon fades, dusk comes. Night comes. But Frankie Hammer doesn't come. Oh, what an innocent I am! How mortified to realize that he was just handing me a line at that dance!

Since I still want to see the fireworks, I decide to go by myself. In the dark I pick my way along the narrow dirt path that leads from Stannard to Middle Beach, then up the hill to Bill Hahn's to find a good seat on the grass for watching the show. But music and light flooding onto the lawn draw me to the resort. I walk up on the patio and look in the large window. On a crowded dance floor, I see Frankie Hammer dancing close with an older girl. The glob of tears I gulp down feels like a rock weight. I cry myself home and into bed. If there are fireworks that night, I neither see nor hear them.

In ninth grade I was lured back to Emanuel Synagogue's religion class when participation in thoughtful discussion replaced a dry textbook. Now, to celebrate Confirmation at the end of tenth grade, there's to be a formal dance. Last summer I met Rick Miller when he spent time at the beach. We hit it off and have been corresponding ever since. I invite him to be my escort to the dance, and he accepts with alacrity. He's a student at Virginia Military

Institute but will come up to Connecticut for the dance and stay to visit relatives. Won't mouths drop when I walk in on the arm of a tall, handsome fellow in full dress uniform! In addition, I can't believe it when my sophisticated classmate Maxanne, whose date drives, offers to pick Rick and me up at my house. Double dating with them will make the evening a complete dream. How I savor the vision!

The big day arrives, and it's now past time for Rick's arrival. Though the doorbell doesn't ring and the phone sits silent, the clock ticks on relentlessly. The time comes to gulp hard and admit that it's happened again—my date is a no-show.

When I can delay no longer, I call Maxanne and tell her that Rick has been stricken with illness and can't make it. She says she is truly sorry, and I say I am, too; I was looking forward to doubling with her and her beau. I hang my gown back in the closet, turn on the radio, and take out a jigsaw puzzle to fill the dragging hours while others are celebrating their Confirmation.

I never know why he didn't come. Three weeks later when the mail brings an envelope with his return address in the corner, I tear it up unopened.

"How can you do that?" Eudy asks. "Don't you want to know what happened?"

"I wanted to know that night," I tell her. "I wanted to know the next night and the night after that. Now it doesn't matter."

"But what if he was in an accident and was hurt?"

"I was hurt. He could have had someone call me so that I only had one puzzle to work on."

Two weeks later I'm in my bedroom at the beach when Mother comes upstairs and announces, "Rick Miller and another boy are here to see you."

"So he doesn't have the courage to face me alone? Please tell him I don't care to see him."

Mother says, "Don't be like that. Go down and talk to

them."

I don't go all the way down but halt several stairs above him. He is wearing no cast, no bandages. Before he can talk, I say quietly, "All my friends believe that you were ill. Please have the courtesy to confirm that story." He nods and opens his mouth, but I've already turned and gone back upstairs. I don't see him or his friend in the area the next day or ever again. When I mature, I'll be more forgiving. Right now the pain is too lingering.

I see such a long road ahead. I must put up with Mother until I'm twenty-one, but I must find a way to put up with myself for a lifetime. Today I will go to the inlet to share the turmoil of the pounding ocean and contribute my tears to its tide.

THE HAIRDO

And yet....And yet she lets me go to Springfield. Springfield, Massachusetts, is about an hour's ride from Hartford. Both cities have active chapters of the B'nai B'rith Youth Organization. Teenage Jewish girls belong to B'nai B'rith Girls and the boys to Aleph Zadik Aleph. BBG girls in one city often date AZA boys in the other, in groups and singly. If they don't drive, they travel back and forth by the convenient train that runs up from New York through New England.

I don't belong to BBG, but my friend Rita, with whom I went to my first nighttime movie, is a member. At a social she has met two Springfield girls who invite her to bring a friend, stay at their homes, and be introduced to some AZA boys for quadruple dating. One of the girls turns out to be the daughter of "Aunt" Laura and "Uncle" Hank, whom I was afraid were getting "dwarfed" so many years ago. I'm specifically invited to stay at their home. Rita and I both hit it off well with our hostesses and our blind dates, and we become an octet all that year for many good times in Springfield and Hartford. Life is looking up.

My beau is a little older than the other boys and is already working in his father's business. In time he transfers to New York, and that's the end of the octet. But in the meantime I've met Len, an outsider, and we start dating. He invites me to a Saturday night prom in Springfield, not a double date. I'm to take the train by myself, stay over at his family's home, and return to Hartford on Sunday. To my astonishment, Mother approves the plan!

She tells me that whenever she was invited anywhere as a girl, her stern Old World father would decree in his Yiddish accent, "Stay chright home." But her timid, fragile mother would lay a hand on his arm and say "*Luzach, luzach,*" or "Let her." Mollie remembers her gratitude to her mother when it's time for her own daughter to go afield.

I spend the morning of the dance in a Hartford beauty salon being topped off with the upswept hairdo which is currently in fashion. It takes tons of hairpins and spray to get my heavy hair to stay on top of my head, but I'm happy with the effect.

Len meets me at the Springfield train station and drives me to his parental home. Just inside the front door I'm confronted with a silent line of five stiff females arranged in steps—three sisters in order of height, their shorter widowed mother, and at the end of the line, the little family dog.

"This is Judy," Len says. Nobody smiles, nobody says a word, and my skull begins to tingle with panic. Finally the dog breaks ranks, runs to me, and as I lower my hand to pet her, she starts licking it. This signal of approval unseals the lips of the Valkyrie. They smile, come toward me, and welcome me into their home. Mercifully, my nerves stop quivering.

Len is a pleasant, good-looking fellow and good company. I enjoy the dance. On the way back to his house, he stops the car at the side of the road, turns off the ignition, and turns toward me. He lifts his arms and saying, "I like your hair natural," he slowly removes every hairpin and runs his hands through the released strands to work out the spray. When my hair has all fallen to my shoulders, he leans over and gently kisses me once. Then he turns the key and drives us home. Even though I'm not in love with him, it's the most romantic thing that has ever happened to me. I have never felt so cherished.

The next morning I return to Hartford on the train, and I don't remember ever seeing him again.

BONJOUR, MES ELEVES

The summer before my second year at Weaver High, I couldn't wait for school to start! Long forgotten were junior high's mandatory home economics course, where I learned the importance of washing the dinner glasses before the china, when the water's hottest and the dish towel driest. Not quite forgotten was sewing class, where the teacher's admittedly faulty cutting of my blouse pattern resulted in an ill-fitting disaster that turned me against ever again inserting a bobbin into my mother's Singer treadle machine. As a junior at Weaver, although I faced Cicero's Orations (UGH!) in third year Latin, I would also start two years of French, a Romance language describing a romantic culture they'd never have understood on the Via Appia. The first words we'd learned in Latin were gladiator, war, and farmer, but our earliest French vocabulary would offer colors like *azur* and foods like *pate de foie gras*. Oh, heaven!

Marie Johnston was born to teach French. She was a plump and pretty middle-aged brunette, happy and full of good will. At the beginning of every class, she beamed upon us all and welcomed, *Bonjour, mes eleves*. She was full of good stories, like the one about hailing a cab in Paris when she was in a hurry to catch a plane. She told the cabbie her airport destination in French, but when he insisted on repeating it several times, she impatiently confirmed in English, "Okay, okay!" Much to her chagrin, she missed her plane when she found herself in a taxi parked on the bank of the Seine. The driver reminded Miss Johnston that she had repeatedly insisted "Au quai! Au quai!!" And the quay is just where he took her.

It is also Miss Johnston who taught us that there is only one way to approach the Arc de Triomphe, which dominates a circle at the crossroads of twelve divergent roads radiating from it like the points of a star. We were to step off the far curb with one arm out stiff, the palm of the hand vertical to stop the traffic rambunctiously scrambling around the plaza, while placing the other hand over our eyes to keep from being scared to death by those oncoming cars. (Nine years later I gratefully survived crossing La Place d'Etoile by literally following her advice.)

Older Latin teacher Gretchen Harper was conscientious, but could anyone in 1948 make more sense of Cicero's harangues in the Roman Senate than of the partisan orations we hear today in our own? Since I'd have all the language credits I needed for college entrance by the time I left Weaver, I respectfully declined Miss Harper's enticements to enjoy my senior year reading poetic Virgil— supposedly the delicious reward for sticking it out with Cicero. When she eventually snagged all six victims she needed for a class, I was relieved of any guilt. Still, Latin may have been the most generous gift of all my education, its roots affording a lifetime of gleaning the definition of many newly-met English words without a dictionary. What a mistake to ever drop it from a curriculum!

Tall, balding Edgar Carrier: now *there* was a man with a sense of humor! When he called me up to his desk to ask why I was failing geometry, I asked in turn—with a straight face— "Mr. Carrier, have you heard me sing?"

"Yes," he kindly responded, "And you have a beautiful voice."

"Well," I proffered, "I'm an artist, not a scientist."

He didn't hit me. The dear man must have had

teenagers of his own, because he even gave me a passing D in the course. Geometry is a boy's subject, anyway; look at the diagrams in the textbook. What did I care about all those trucks driving up and down vectors?

Willard Green and Weston Brockway of the music faculty were a kind of their own. Every girl in glee club, choir, and band had a crush on one or both of them. And how could I help liking F. Elliot Larrabee, who announced to my whole homeroom class that I reminded him of a poem about "the girl with sunlight in her hair," even though I sat away from the window?

I finally made friendships at Weaver. My circle either sang, played an instrument, and/or wrote for the school newspaper, *The Lookout*. A small group of us were opera buffs. Periodically we'd select a libretto and a score at the library and take them to someone's home to follow along as we played a record of the full opera. Each of us claimed a role according to our range, and after we'd practiced with the record and libretto, our pianist would accompany us as we reached for translucent beauty in a performance with only ourselves as rapturous audience. Sadly, we had no means of preserving that effort.

Next, beauty took a back seat to mischief as we created a hilarious ad-libbed spoof of the work. Often one or more of us ended up gasping with laughter, unable to continue our role. I can vividly picture the tall frame of our bass, Charlie Reilly—later known to the world as Charles Nelson Reilly—collapsing in an articulated fall, first to his knees and then flat onto my folks' Oriental rug, suffused in gales of laughter.

These were the rays of light that managed to break through the storm cloud of adolescence.

THE BLESSING OF HOPE

Although the student body of my high school class was about one third Jewish, my dearest friend and rival for soprano solos in all the choirs was Irish. As Hope Hailey and I visited each other back and forth, I did not tell my parents that she lived a considerable bus ride away, a few doors down from the city jail in a predominantly Black neighborhood. When Hope's church choir needed another strong soprano to sing Faure's Requiem at Easter, I began rehearsing with them weekly. In that choir loft I received another great gift—a lifelong love of the exalted music of Roman Catholic masses. *Oy*, if my parents only knew!

One day when Hope was on her way to visit me at my house, she was struck down by a bus on Albany Avenue and taken to the hospital instead. After she was sent home to recuperate from her injuries, I went to see her. She was excited that I brought a carton of the ice cream she loved— the first food she'd been able to stomach for days. She sat up in bed and devoured the whole carton right then and there.

Then she turned to me. "You know, Judy, *I* know you're shy, but when you look away from kids in the hall at school and don't talk to them, they think you're stuck-up because you're a star."

Oh, how wrong! I always thought *they* would snub *me* because I didn't fit in. The very next day I mustered up all my courage, marched up to the impressively successful and attractive girl I most thought wouldn't ever bother with me and said, "Hi, Adele, I love your dress. It goes so well with your coloring." To my happy astonishment, she looked directly into my eyes, smiled broadly, and responded, "You don't think it's too dressy for school?" She cared what I thought! We chatted briefly before class, and she sounded as if she'd have always been happy to talk to me. What a revelation! After that I rarely looked away from anybody. All my life I will be grateful that my friend Hope loved me enough to tell me a life-changing truth.

HOW I LEARNED TO SMOKE
(and How I Paid for It)

My sixteen-year-old friends, Eudy, Rhoda, and Softy, were already smoking an occasional cigarette, but I had no great urge to join the crowd. During a visit one afternoon when my folks were out, the girls left the remains of their cigarettes in the little cut-glass rectangular ash trays that sat next to the elaborate silver Ronson lighter on my parents' coffee table (now always appropriately centered in front of the sofa). With nothing to hide, I had not yet emptied the ashes and butts into the monogrammed silver jaws of the silent butler, another of their wedding gifts, when my parents came home. They spotted what they thought was incriminating evidence, and Mother went into a tizzy.

"You're smoking!" she exploded.

"No," I tried to reassure her, "I don't smoke. These are Rhoda's and Eudy's butts." Turning to my father as the more reasonable parent, I continued, "Right now I'm not interested in smoking. I will not do it behind your back. Obviously, if I ever change my mind, I will have taken some puffs of the girls' cigarettes to see if it's something I care to do. But if I want to continue, I promise I will ask you for the first full cigarette." Dad at least knew that I considered a promise sacred, but Mother didn't understand about that and remained blazing mad.

I felt no need to "keep up" with my friends, and I have no memory of why, with no intent to emulate them, on rare occasion I did try a puff of someone's cigarette. Just taking a little smoke into my mouth and letting it right out again, the taste was pleasant and the activity felt sophisticated. I think the sophistication was what got me. Or maybe it was a different kind of camaraderie on a day that summer.

On that bright, sunny morning Mother, Dad, and I had been invited to sail off the coast of New London, Connecticut, on the Swayes' cabin cruiser. Uncle Larry and Aunt Sarah were also included. As we started across the dock, Mother looked down and spied the lapping water under the wooden slats at her feet. She stopped dead in her tracks and whimpering, "I can't do this," backed up until she regained solid ground. Esther Swaye and Aunt Sarah were admirably sympathetic. Realizing that Mother was really too panicked to board the boat, our hostess brightly proposed that the three of them go shopping and meet the fellows for lunch in town after they docked. When I was given leeway to join whichever group I chose, I didn't hesitate. I had always considered men's conversation and character so much more substantial than women's.

The sail on the sparkling water was delightful, and my companions were so respectful of my contributions to the conversation that as usual, I felt like one of the guys. When my father took out his package of Pall Malls, without a conscious decision I asked, "May I have one?" just as I'd promised. I saw the inimitable Horowitz twinkle hop into both brothers' eyes at the same time. Dad tilted his pack at me, I took a cigarette, and as soon as it hit my lips, Uncle Larry's pocket lighter leapt into flame at its tip. No problem with permission here. If they were amused that I didn't inhale the smoke, they didn't let on.

I think Dad now felt that he'd acquired a comrade in arms against Mother's disapproval of smoking. As soon as we finished lunch with the ladies, he casually offered me another cigarette across the table. Uncle Larry, his eyes again dancing, lit it just as fast as the first. Mother's eyes almost leaped out of her head and anger rouged her face, but unable to explode in front of the Swayes, she expressed only surprise. Aunt Sarah's expression said she read Mother's fury but would not condemn her own husband's complicity in the cause.

Later at home, after Mother read the Riot Act to Dad, she turned on me and issued her executive order: "I forbid you to smoke!"

Neither of my poor parents ever caught on to the effect that word had on me or that I refused to diminish myself by lying. As once before, I offered Mother a choice. "Does that mean you only want me to do it behind your back, or may I do it in front of you as well? Because I am going to smoke." And I did. Both places.

I'd heard tales of girls getting nauseous and dizzy trying to inhale, and I was in no hurry to do that. But one day I called Eudy and said, "I have the time today to be sick and recover. Would you like to teach me to inhale?" I walked to her house, and we sat on the cement steps out front. She showed me how to take the smoke into my lungs and then let it out. Were we both surprised when I did it right and nothing uncomfortable happened! I almost wished it had, to test if this was something I really wanted to do. But it was too easy. I went on to smoke for fourteen years before I quit to avoid inviting cancer. Fifty years after that, when my doctor placed a stent in an artery narrowed by plaque, he laid the major blame on the doorstep of all those old cigarettes.

THE WALLPAPER WARS

The wallpaper in the childhood room I shared with Roan featured a series of charming red-roofed cottages staggered between rows of trees, all set against a white background. Often while lying or sitting on my bed against the wall, I imagined walking through the trees from a house of which I was the mistress to deliver freshly baked cookies to a friend's home in another row. I rarely took the direct route; more often I meandered through several stands of trees and houses before arriving at my friend's. Either I made the trip solely with my eyes or traced it with my finger, and I confess once with a pencil line which was ruefully erased after a maternal eruption.

From this setting in the summer when I was nine years old, my folks sent Roan and me to overnight Camp Woodstock for a week. I wasn't homesick for even a minute; I loved being away. But when we returned home a week later, I came to a shocked halt at the threshold of our bedroom. My precious realm of houses and trees had vanished from walls now covered with Wedgewood blue paper etched with silver ferns. So that's why we were packed off to camp! To be out of the way while this betrayal was consummated!

The new wall covering was pretty enough, but without consultation or advance notice, I felt forcibly shoved from childhood into young ladyhood before I was ready. The décor *was* now more appropriate for Roan's age, but the surprise was Mother's when her secret plan produced not the two pleased smiles she'd envisioned but my long face of mourning for my lost neighborhood.

So now seven years later, when the family is evicted and has to move, Mother has brought home a sample of the wallpaper she's selected for my Hebron Street room. Roan will be away at college during the week, but since she's engaged to Howard and he's doing his Army stint in Texas, she won't be in the dating scene on campus. She'll be home every weekend. Mother and Dad have grown too old to be comfortable in a double bed, and I'm informed that they're going to move their whole oppressive dark mahogany bedroom suite into the back room. I'm to occupy that room by myself for five nights and share it with Roan for two. Our modern maple twin set will go in the front bedroom for my parents, and I'll be stuck with a roomful of gloomy behemoths and a weekend bed partner.

Mother unrolls the sample of the wallpaper she's chosen to backdrop this scene. IT'S HIDEOUS! Down a lurid yellow background race stripes of choking, mammoth-leafed jungle vines bearing huge white flowers in succulent full bloom.

I tell Mother, "It's so humid it will make me nauseous!"

She huffs, "Then *you* go pick a paper!"

In joyous disbelief, I take the bus downtown to the wallpaper store and come home with a sample scroll of white wall covering scattered with off-white polka dots and delicate pink rosebuds.

Mother scoffs, "Impractical!" at the white background (the same as on my childhood houses) and forthwith has the paperhangers install the jungle. It may not make me nauseous, as high humidity usually does, but every morning emerging into consciousness in the depths of the Amazon brings on profuse sweating. Once dressed, I avoid the room like the plague until I'm ready to sleep again. My weekend bedmate has no complaints, but I yowl enough for the two of us. When I'm miserable, I can sure make my parents miserable. Whether it's the force of my adolescent persuasion or because my folks miss their double bed, within a few months they decree that we will switch rooms. I am now reunited with my lighter twin-bed set, and gentle sunlight falls through the windows upon the delicate little bouquets of multicolored flowers against a pastel green background which Mother chose for her own walls.

Even when I leave for college, my parents don't immediately return to the front room. I'm still coming back for the odd weekend and for the summer. And then when I'm invited into their tropical lair to report on an evening's date, Tarzan and Jane seem happy back in their old bed while I surreptitiously lick off the first drops of unbecoming sweat forming over my upper lip.

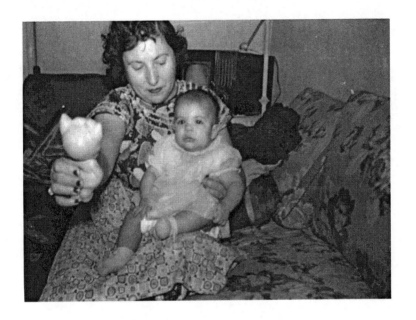

Mother with baby Robin

Little Aunt Rose in Sedona, AZ

Jody, you're so bold!

Roan

Grampa

Big Lois and Aunt Sarah

Daddy

Mint, a sawed off Peppermint

Papa & Mama Fenster, Seymour & Judy,
Mollie & Dan Horowitz

The church on Main Street, Newington

Lucy Robbins Welles Library, Newington
I was elected to their Board.

Uncle Lou sang dye-dee-dye

Seymour's own office building

Lillian and Louis Lovins

Judy and Richard's Wedding Day

The crabapple tree

Susie and Mike in the West Hartford back yard

Searching

LEARNING AND GROWING

I'm sitting alone in the back seat of my parents' car. In the front Mother and Dad are having an exclusionary conversation, as is their wont, sending me off into my lonely dreams. Only today I'm not dreaming. I'm on my way to the University of Connecticut to matriculate as a freshman. A question jabs me: What am I doing here? I never decided to go to college! It was written when I was born, and I never imagined any alternative.

I'm not distressed, though. For one thing, I'm going to be living away from that couple in the front seat, taking the one-hour bus ride back to Hartford only often enough to convince them that they're not unloved.

Roan is no longer at UConn. Married at the end of her sophomore year, she's now living in Boston with her husband, expecting their first child. At UConn, however, I'll see the fellows she dated in high school before Howard came along. After a delay to fulfill their mandatory military service requirement, veterans have been belatedly flooding the campus under the GI Bill. I will often have to correct one of my sister's former beaux, "No, I am not *Roan's sister*; I am *Judy*." But those who hankered after the slim blonde won't be interested in the pudgy redhead. I will have to find my own admirers.

The process is jump-started when I'm actually invited to join a sorority—yes, really! Do you believe it? I'm assigned two benevolent pledge tasks by my new Phi Sigma Sigma sisters. I think of the three Jewish fraternities on campus as The Thinkers, The Drinkers, and The Sex Fiends. Into the middle of the first group's Saturday night party I'm sent with two other Phi Sig pledges. Our instructions are to make ourselves at home without uttering a word. Unescorted and wearing our mandated freshman beanies, we are quickly noticed. When asked who we are, where we come from, and why we are there, we may only reply, "Women who are frightened by bears have children with bare feet." This, of course, produces much merriment and enough interest that the Phi Sigma Delta boys learn our names from our Phi Sigma Sigma sisters, and some call for dates. Yes, even the fat one is called. On campus it's Freshman Rush and Sophomore Slump, and we are the new girls in town.

I perform my other pledge task alone—singing the sorority song on the college radio station. This immediately leads to my being offered my own weekly musical show with announcer Bo and piano accompanist Gene. My theme song is "Over the Rainbow," just like Judy Garland. My two cohorts and I have a great time with the show all my freshman year, and my name becomes known on campus. Now, that's the kind of hazing fraternity men ought to learn!

UConn's administration, with its own bizarre sense of humor, has drummed up some pretty wicked hazing of its own. It's called Registration Day. In the auditorium, students sit at long rows of tables with course catalogues, marking on blank schedules the days and times of classes we wish to take. I'm aware of no mentors or faculty present to help freshmen this first time around. When we've managed to fit a schedule together, we're to take it up to the stage, where volunteer fraternity brothers register us into the classes. The place looks like a poorly run Election Day, with staggered easels onstage indicating which sections of which courses are still open. Just as I finish fitting all the pieces of my academic jigsaw puzzle together and am heading up the aisle to register, a volunteer approaches an easel and crosses out a line. He calls out, "Tuesday-Thursday math 101 is now closed." Since freshman math is required, I stop in my tracks, scoot over to the nearest table, and re-juggle French, philosophy, landscape gardening, and physical education to fit in the Monday-Wednesday math section. (I'm so glad I've passed the test to exempt me from freshman English!) Thank heavens nothing else I need closes before I get my reworked schedule up to the promised land. This precludes the need to start at Square One again and perhaps even have to substitute a lesser choice for a desired subject. What a way to run a university!

New sorority and fraternity pledges must wait until sophomore year to move into the private Greek houses. I'm just as happy, because I probably learn more in Sprague independent dorm than I do in the classroom. Instead of being cloistered with girls who share my own familiar background, I'm living among a population whose diversity fascinates me. I spend more time sitting tailor fashion on dorm beds, asking and answering questions about our differing upbringing and cultures, than I do studying textbooks. That is when I feel I am really growing—and nobody can close out the course!

THE CAFETERIA

The University of Connecticut in Storrs, Connecticut, was founded in 1881 as Storrs Agricultural School. In 1949 its Aggie component still prides itself on the farm products it provides the three university cafeterias. When today's students weary of this rich cafeteria food, there are only two alternatives. We are forbidden to cook in our own rooms. To enforce that ban, the dorm police conduct surprise searches, and invariably another clandestine hotplate is pulled from a giant-size Kotex box at the back of a dark closet. Since the students can't seem to outsmart the snoops, there's not a whole lot of home cooking going on.

Instead, on cold evenings the gals in Sprague buy wrapped Italian grinders at a closeout price just before the mom-and-pop general store on South Campus closes. We lay them on our window sills overnight and devour them cold for breakfast the next morning.

Or we can, always with a buddy, stand on a certain corner on the road that runs through campus to Willimantic and look hungry. Without our raising a thumb, southbound drivers understand our need and stop to offer a ride into Willi. In town at The Rock Garden, we enjoy live jazz while eating. At the historical Hooker House hotel dining room, we're told the doorbell still imbedded in the wall next to each of our booths once summoned female company in case pleasure other than food was desired.

After dinner, Willi's one movie theater offers a postwar film with such predictable dialogue that the audience recites the lines along with the actors. The notable exception is Up in Arms starring Danny Kaye, the hysterically funny new star. No way could we anticipate or replicate his hilarious gibberish!

Afterward, again with no need for a signal, accommodating northbound motorists stop at a nearby corner to offer rides back to UConn. Lord, let our parents never know the chances we take! A friend and I are offered a ride one night by a couple of kind Samaritans, but only after the dark car gets going do previously unnoticed empty beer cans start rolling around our feet. Though the Samaritans seem perfectly sober, we hold our breath all the way back to campus. Mercifully, years into the future a choice of interesting restaurants will be built on university grounds, a regular bus will run between Storrs and Willi, and fewer tales will need to remain untold.

In present conditions, we most often resign ourselves to the campus cafeterias' offerings. Waiting to reach the serving counter, we girls stand in line knitting argyle socks for our fathers, brothers, uncles, cousins, and boyfriends. This is The Year of the Argyle Sock, and the cafeteria scene is enlivened at every mealtime by colorful yarns dangling on bobbins from each coed's four needles.

Standing behind me as I knit in line one day is Nortie, the Weaver friend elevated to boyfriend last year and now retired from that position. As we chat, he proclaims with newly acquired *savoir faire,* "A girl isn't socially acceptable unless she plays bridge and tennis." He later marries a girl who does both, while I learn and then drop bridge, finding more enjoyment in using the undeniably needed smarts to read a book. As for tennis, after mandatory instruction in P.E., I can manage a leisurely game if I have a tolerant opponent. So at least I half pass muster.

In spring all salt shakers suddenly vanish from the

cafeteria tables. The girls steal them to make salt water in their beer steins received as prom favors. Everyone knows that brine applied to the body encourages a better tan while sunbathing in the sheltered dorm courtyards. Then why, on a bright, sunny day, instead of showing off the hard-earned results, are so many copper-skinned beauties on their way to class wrapped in raincoats? I'll tell you a little secret: since the university dress code forbids shorts in the classroom, under those raincoats is hidden their oh, so socially acceptable tennis wear.

A BAD SEASON

The summer of 1950 is a heartbreaking time. In a darkened car parked outside my home, with gloomy rain falling like a clichéd movie backdrop, my cousin Melvin informs me that my adored Uncle Larry, fifty years old, has inoperable cancer.

A hospital bed is brought into the den at Uncle Larry's home, where he is visited by loving friends and family as he slides toward his life's end. My father goes over to shave him every day, but one weekend when Dad is distracted in his workshop retreat, an electric saw nearly slices his thumb off. After the doctor bandages it thickly, it looks like a cartoon character's big round sore thumb, but it's not funny. Dad continues to groom Uncle Larry every day. But even with an electric shaver, the process is now so taxing that to spare him doing it twice, I shave Dad every morning before he leaves the house. I'm proud to be useful and feel as privileged as when I sweep up sawdust in his basement workshop.

My father loves his brother deeply and is grieving painfully watching him die. I love my father deeply and am painfully watching him grieve. I can find no joy in eating, and before the summer's over, I've lost thirty-five pounds.

A FORK IN THE ROAD

When I return to school in September, my roommate and I settle into our room in the new Phi Sigma Sigma dorm. UConn has just built large integrated dormitories to replace the homey but exclusive private cottages of the "Greek" community. It has clustered the sororities on South Campus, juxtaposing affiliated and independent wings in cruciform buildings. Every wing has its own large lounge on the first floor, and Phi Sig must now staff its own kitchen and dining room. If we don't pledge enough members to fill our upstairs rooms, we'll be obliged to house non-members, thus diluting the mix and compromising any sorority confidentiality.

In the summer's furious building boom, grass and trees have been uprooted from the surrounding gentle hills and haven't yet been replaced. Without them to hold the ground, rain has turned the area into a sea of squishy mud. We girls must step very carefully onto wooden boards laid down for our passage into and out of our new dorm, dodging construction equipment still on site.

The food truck parked outside to feed the remaining builders becomes famous for its tasty hot breakfast fare. Before early classes it's as popular with coeds as with workmen. I enjoy breakfast standing at the truck before trekking to my 8:00 a.m. English class in an Aggie building clear across campus. Then it's too long a walk back over the renowned rolling hills of Connecticut to the muck of South

Campus before my next class. Instead, I elect to hang out in the library in mid-campus, where I spend the time studying and smoking in the downstairs ladies' lounge and forget about lunch.

After the harrowing summer when grief stole my appetite for food, I've returned to school with a new, slimmer shape, and skipping lunches preserves it. This makes me essentially a new girl on campus again, attracting some attention the boys usually only focus on incoming freshmen. My Phi Sig sisters, suffering from Sophomore Slump, are not amused. Some of these "ladies" even go so far as to snidely conjecture how I might be earning such popularity. Where is the warm welcome I felt when I was fat?

I upset the sisters again later in the year. Sponsored by Hillel religious and social center, once a year the three Jewish fraternities and two sororities compete in presenting original skits with a common theme. Our gals won the award for best show the last two times. Because last year I wrote and directed the skit Phi Sig pledges traditionally mount in-house for the full-fledged sisters, now I'm asked to fashion our entry into the Hillel contest. Things go well until one of the most popular girls in the house consistently fails to show up for rehearsals. Because she's threatening our winning streak, when she ignores my pleas to commit to the project, I try to recast her role. The sorority swoops to the defense of happy-go-lucky Joy and frowns on *too serious* Judy. Joy keeps her role but doesn't change her ways. With truncated rehearsals and poor morale (of course not because the winning fraternity's entry is more clever), we fail to retain the award. I've lost friends, but oh, have I learned a lesson in politics!

I do still have some buddies left in the Phi Sig house. Three of us form the property committee for the Theater Department's production of The Glass Menagerie. In our quest for empty liquor bottles to fill with whiskey-looking tea for the set's home bar, we know just where to go. On a Sunday morning I'm bent double over the dumpster behind a fraternity house, triumphantly waving "dead soldiers" as I fish them out. After I've retrieved an ample stash, my accomplices suddenly roll startled eyes toward the edge of the lot to indicate a clutch of adults frigidly staring at us. Oh, my lord, we've forgotten that today is Parents Visiting Day, and we're definitely not the image their sons want them to take home! We turn to explain what we're doing, but the parents are already gone in a huff and a puff. We can't help it; we collapse in laughter.

The rehearsal schedule for Menagerie turns out to be a blessing when a flu epidemic hits the campus. Students are dropping by the dozens, and every night there are a few more empty chairs in the Phi Sig dining room. The girls have either taken their misery upstairs to bed or have gone home to suffer it out. But Sibyl, Lorraine and I have never felt better! When we're not studying, our hours are crammed with hunting down props and attending rehearsals. We have no time to be sick, and having fun seems to bolster the immune system! All three of us survive the entire season of contagion without a single symptom.

For my elective class in play directing, I've chosen Tennessee Williams' one-act Lady of Larkspur Lotion, casting myself as the put-upon landlady. The campus reviewer kindly says that in that role "Judy Horowitz was so tough I sure would hate to owe her back rent!"

I wish I were that tough in real life. When I wasn't invited to join a high school sorority I felt as forlorn as the legendary little match girl, on the outside looking in. What a thrill it was to be welcomed into Phi Sigma Sigma at UConn! My first year was validating and exciting, but now I'm beginning to wonder what I was yearning for when looking in from the outside. Yes, I enjoy some friendships in the exclusive club, but when I'm stimulated by new ideas in class discussion and reading, I can't bring that back into the dorm. The interest there in boys, clothes, parties, and status seems overriding. And I'm hardly getting the feeling of bonding I thought sorority was about. I'm beginning to suspect I've misunderstood what was being offered. I'm probably not the right clay for this model, either. Am I really where I want to be?

There's another question demanding an answer. Since childhood I've toyed with the idea of becoming a writer, but I never wanted to starve in a garret until I published. This year because of my success in Cecil Hinkle's inaugural History of Theater course, he's hired me to help grade his second semester students' papers. Theater and writing are both inviting fields, but what *is* it I want to do with my life?

For my sophomore class in creative writing, I pen a short story titled Satan in the Subway, which is as gloomy as I'm feeling. As my instructor passes our papers back in class, he tells me, "You remind me of Rilke, but your writing is pretty abstruse." Why do I never ask for an appointment with him, ask him to elaborate, ask for direction? Instead without further consultation, I decide that I must study journalism to tame my abstruse style. Although I've written for my school newspapers since seventh grade and earned membership in the Quill and Scroll student journalism society, I've never had formal training. Now I discover that the top journalism school in the Northeast is at Boston University. It's only two hours from Hartford, but it costs four hundred dollars annual tuition instead of UConn's in-state one hundred twenty-five dollars.

Time is running out to settle on a major course of study, and after sampling other fields (including landscape gardening, where I learned never to plant an umbrella catalpa tree in my front yard), writing seems to be what I'd most like to do with my life. Even more motivating, I'm so sick of this isolated rural campus overrun with teens sporting raincoats, tennis racquets, and frivolous minds! I want to see men walking toward me full of purpose, wearing suits, and carrying briefcases. Day after day the only grownups I now see, and then briefly, are teachers and housemothers. I want to go to a city bustling with all kinds of adults and ideas, with museums and galleries, theaters and concert halls. I want to be part of challenging exchanges with minds beyond adolescence.

In spite of the difference in tuition, my parents allow me to apply for admission to B.U.'s School of Public Relations and Communication, and I'm accepted for the fall of 1951!

I know that Boston is a treasure house of opportunities where money will be better spent than on the Hellenic life with which I'm now disillusioned. Although there's a Phi Sig chapter at B.U., sorority would seem superfluous there. At the beginning of second semester, the officers of UConn's chapter propose an eye-rolling assessment on each member for expensive Chippendale furniture to fill the spacious lounge we've been saddled with. Refusing to tap my parents for it—so far I've paid all costs of sorority with my own earnings—I go inactive. Even though I must continue to remain in the same edifice till summer, it's a surprising relief to be free once more!

I have learned much. Now I feel that I'm leaving the land of what I am not and am on my way to finding who I am.

I SHOULDA BEEN A BOY

When I was dating Ralph from Hartford High in my sophomore year at Weaver, we often double-dated with his buddy Marvin. Marv and I became warm friends. But after the night Ralph tried to French kiss me goodnight—that nasty process Roan had told me about!—I cut him off forever. I rarely had occasion to bump into Marv after that, and I was delighted to discover him at UConn. We renewed our friendship as he often came to pick up Charlyn, a dormmate of mine, and the three of us had a great relationship.

One Sunday morning in my second year at our transportation-deprived campus, Marv showed up at the Phi Sig house with a car he'd just bought. He led me out to the street where it was parked and pointed to the passenger's side. He said, "See that? That seat belongs to you. If you ever need a ride anywhere, you just call me and I'll come for you." I tucked that sweet offer in the back of my mind in case of emergency, but I had no intention of imposing on my friend.

Later that spring, Marv came to a Sunday morning Hillel brunch hosted at the Phi Sig house. Charlyn wasn't there, and after the brunch Marv and I walked some way away from the house and sat on a white rail fence, chatting. When the conversation rolled around to summer plans, suddenly I saw a brainstorm hit my friend. "Hey!" he practically shouted, "Let's you and I hitchhike cross-country this summer! We can stop in towns along the way and work a while to make money, then take off to the next place!"

Vagabonding! What a delicious idea! It brought joy just to envision it, and I laughed with delight. But depression followed swiftly, strangling all the carefree visions which presented themselves. Platonic friendship is all well and good, but it's careless to completely forget that your buddy is of a different gender. "Marv," I almost sobbed, "I can't! I'M A GIRL!"

"So?"

"Girls can't do those things. Especially traveling with a male. Even though *they* know they're just friends, her reputation would be destroyed."

He cocked his head to one side and pondered the thought. "Yeah, I guess you're right. But it sure would be fun."

It wasn't fair. Boys could do all sorts of great things that weren't proper for girls, even if the gal was perfectly strong and capable enough for it. Why *shouldn't* a girl play drums or hitchhike cross-country with a friend? While a boy didn't have to worry about his reputation, a girl's was wrapped around her neck like an albatross. I was suffused with disappointment and resentment. For long years after that I wished I'd been born a boy, and I hoped I would never pass such hardship down to a daughter.

Fortunately, by the time my baby Susie came along, the world was changing.

DANCING ON TABLES

Many girls who didn't have a date for the weekend took the bus home late Friday rather than stay on campus feeling chagrined and bored. But early in my very first semester, an upperclass gal related that often after the bus left, the hall phone rang and a perfectly nice fellow asked if anyone in the dorm would like to be his Saturday night date. "It might start your social life rolling," she advised. The first weekend I stayed on campus it happened. I accepted the invitation, enjoyed a pleasant evening at a Phi Ep party with a likeable guy, and a few other dates followed.

It wasn't long before I met Denny in just that way. For some reason our paths hadn't crossed at the party I'd crashed as a sorority pledge task, even though he was the social chairman of Phi Sigma Delta. On a later weekend he'd delayed too long arranging a date and at the last minute called my dorm. Luckily I was the one who answered the phone.

Denny was one of those rare special people I think of as Salt of the Earth. I was intrigued by his intelligence, his interest in photography and medicine, tales of his Navy service, his decency, humanity, and caring for other people. He was easygoing and made me feel relaxed. He was responsible; you could count on him. And he was fun. I dated him more than anyone else during my two years at UConn. I thought the world of him, but I was too dumb to fall in love with him. Or did I just have too much unfinished business in finding out who I wanted to be?

Denny wanted to pin me. But I couldn't do that, because wearing a fellow's fraternity pin was the precursor to wearing his engagement ring and then marriage, and my heart wasn't leading me there. I was on my way to Boston to open a whole new chapter of my life, and I was in love only with the idea of freedom.

We had a deep discussion of what we each wanted out of life, and he was so sensible. But when he asked me about my hopes, I answered, "I don't want to be sensible! I want to be a little crazy! When the music starts, I want to jump up and dance on tables!" He tried to explain how little satisfaction that would bring in the end, but we were in two different places. We agreed that once I went to Boston, we would stop seeing each other. I have always hoped that he quickly met a woman who had no need to dance on tables.

THE THESPIAN

I arrive at Boston University in September 1951. How different their registration procedure is from UConn's! At B.U.'s School of Public Relations and Communications in Copley Square, I'm immediately connected with an advisor who discusses the requirements I need to fulfill and electives I might choose. He walks me through the process, and I'm in and out in short order instead of struggling by myself for almost a whole day. I feel welcomed rather than abandoned.

Shortly before my last semester at UConn, a new thought suddenly came barreling down the pike: *In two years I'm going to be voting age, and I have no basis for making wise choices. I've always heard that communism is bad, but do I know why? For that matter, what do I really understand about capitalism or any other economic or political system?* I couldn't bear the thought of being an ignorant voter and was angry that the school system had let me get so far without the tools necessary for intelligent citizenship.

If I'm going to exercise my right to vote—which I'm eager to do—I'd better educate myself, I thought. Because I was transferring out, I didn't need to fill UConn's specific graduation requirements and could use my last semester to take electives. Peter Schroeder taught an engrossing comparative government course, rocking on his heels with his thumbs hooked in his belt, snarling when construction noise under our classroom window interrupted his transmission of important information. Now at B.U. I have the chance to study comparative economics. Still, journalism is my joy, and I'm excited about faculty who've actually worked in the field.

I also continue my immersion in theater by enrolling in the George Gershwin Theater Workshop, mentored by Richard Rogers and "Uncle Oscar" Hammerstein. They come to watch our work and encourage us once a year.

Two performances are especially memorable to me. Just before curtain time for Down in the Valley by Kurt Weil, I'm joshing with another cast member while ironing my costume in the greenroom. He feigns that he's about to attack me, and I raise the iron as if to fend him off. It swings inward and sizzles the tender inside of my forearm. I want to scream, but I know The Show Must Go On. I apply a generous gob of Vaseline and a gauze wrapping from the first aid kit and get myself on stage in my ironed costume when I'm due.

In the square dance scene, the caller intones:
"Ladies bow, gents bow under.
Hold your holts and swing like thunder!"
Two ladies alternate with two gents in each square. We gals link arms across the guys' shoulders, jump off the ground onto their arms twined behind our arched backs, lift our heels and are swung in mid-air. As my arm strains across my gentleman's shoulders, the pressure tortures my burn, but I know I'm a true actress when I manage to keep smiling and singing till the show's over. It will take ten years for the scarlet imprint of the iron's sole plate to fade to a gradually paler rose, then pink and then disappear completely from my inner arm.

Even a later narrow escape doesn't discourage the thespian in me. In our production of Raggedy Ann and Andy I am cast as Mint, "a sawed-off Peppermint" as played by a redheaded fellow who towers over me in height. We give a matinee performance in a ward of Children's Hospital surrounded by young patients' beds wheeled into a circle around us. The choreography calls for me to run up a tall stepladder helter-skelter, flinging my legs out to the sides as I leave each step, and at the top turn with a flounce of the poufy white petticoat under my flared red skirt and sit abruptly. When I whirl around and plunk my saucy little bottom on the top stair, I'm stunned to find myself face to face with a steel traction bar just inches from my eyes! Again I keep smiling, hiding my terror at the near miss from the young patients whose laughter is so rewarding. This acting business can be dangerous! But I love it. I've loved make believe ever since I stayed glued to Let's Pretend, and now I am a part of it.

WHAT'S MINE IS MINE

When I was a little girl, my grandmother Anna Horowitz had a delicate Victorian fan made of thin, lacy ivory decorated with frilly white satin ribbon and demure, hand-painted pink rosebuds. I was so crazy about that fan that one day when my family was visiting in Brooklyn, Grandma gave it to me for my very own. It is the only gift I can ever remember her giving me. But when we got back to Hartford, Mother made me give it up. She decreed that I was so young (again!) that I'd probably break or lose the fan; therefore she would safeguard it for me until I was old enough to care for it myself. She took my treasure from me, folded it up, and placed it in the bottom left-hand drawer of her mahogany dressing table.

Often when Mother was out playing Mah Jongg or shopping, I secretly visited that drawer and took out the fan to gaze upon its beauty. I'd gently open it out, wave it before my face, and for a short time revel in knowing that it was mine. Then I'd quietly put it back under Mother's control. As time passed, the surreptitious visits stopped, but I never forgot my lovely fan lying in Mother's drawer, and one day the time came to claim my right of possession.

"I'd like to have my fan now," I told Mother. She looked surprised, as if she'd forgotten all about it, but she didn't argue with me. We walked to her dressing table, and she opened the bottom drawer. There was no fan there. Yet

Mother didn't seem upset.

"Now, where can it be?" she mused.

"Did you possibly put it in a different drawer?" I asked her.

"No," she said, "I never open this drawer to take anything out." Then she added vaguely, "I don't know where it is." I insisted she go through the rest of the drawers in her bedroom, but the fan did not turn up, and Mother continued to deny knowing what happened to it. It is possible, of course, that one of our Long Lane maids had helped herself to the fan while dusting, but none of those girls ever stole anything from us. Mother supervised them closely. The lack of privacy in their common-use bedroom/playroom, presented no sure hiding place. The young women had no visitors, and they didn't go out unescorted. So how did my beautiful treasure and sweet memento of my grandmother disappear? It would be uncomfortable to wonder about someone I needed to trust.

I finally had to accept that the cherished fan was gone forever. The hollow space that a vibrating apprehension had been scraping out within me while we searched now filled with the heavy mist of loss. I never saw my beloved fan again, and in the far recesses of my mind, though I have forgiven much, I have never stopped mourning the gift that was so precious to me.

There were only a few other things at home that I valued highly. In my Rawson School years when I played at Joan Porter's house, I was suffused with envy over a fat stuffed panda sitting on her bed. Such pandas were common among girls my age. I longed to have one of my own, but nobody remembered my persistent requests when Chanukah or a birthday came around. Then in my sophomore year at UConn, one of David Elovitz's friends at Worcester Polytech invited me to their fraternity dance. On the big night, the guys all slept in a nearby hotel and turned over their rooms in the frat house to their dates. As I set my overnight bag down in Rob's room, I caught sight of my prom favor sitting on the bed—would you believe, a fat, stuffed, brightly white-and-black panda! Yay! At the age of eighteen, I finally had my own bear! But since my shared narrow room in the Phi Sig dorm was already crowded with our necessities, there was no space for Panda to be comfortable. The day after the dance, he joined Lucy, the chintz doll I had won at the Saybrook carnival, on my bed in my parents' house.

A couple of years later on a weekend home from B.U., I entered my bedroom and saw that Lucy and Panda no longer sat atop my bedspread. When I asked Mother where they were, she confessed this story:

Roan came to visit one afternoon with her toddler, Robin. To keep the child amused while mother and daughter chatted, Mother gave Robin both my lucky girl and long-awaited panda to play with. Robbie is not a destructive child, but she is a child, and when Mother and Roan checked on her in the sunroom later, they found scattered on the floor the stuffing that was somehow spilling out of the two creatures. Before the poor torn things could make more of a mess, both were whisked into the trash. Later in the afternoon Robbie was attracted to my collection of long-playing symphonic records. She removed many of them from their cardboard jackets, placed them under the sunroom rug and danced vigorously on top of them. The shards of those records were also quickly thrown out. Somehow Mother forgot to tell me of all these losses until I came home and noticed my things missing. My father's constant admonition, "Respect your mother," ringing in my ears, I fumed that in my family respect was strictly a one-way street.

In time I also learned that the childhood books I'd envisioned passing down to a daughter of my own—my Maida series; Beverly Gray, Girl Reporter; and Judy—had been gifted to my niece. No one had asked me if that was okay. When I asked for them back to save for my own child, no one knew where they'd gone to.

I heard Miss Crayon shout crazily, "We must learn to share!" and I remembered my childhood vow to hold my belongings close. But you see that was not always possible, and how could I have suspected that my treasures lay in the hands of a steward who never quite understood that they were MINE?

THE COMMAND

When the students of the George Gershwin Theater Workshop convene for the first time in 1951, I find myself sitting next to Freddie B. He's short like me, middlin' Jewish like me, and we have the same irreverent sense of humor. We start dating, and in short order we are officially going steady. When he clasps around my neck a seed pearl choker from his father's jewelry business, I feel calmly anchored for the first time in my life.

Often when he comes to the theater, Freddie brings me a single carnation purchased from a street vendor. (I love this city!) In return, every once in a while I surprise him with one of the Chunky chocolate squares he loves. After rehearsals when he walks me back to my dorm, Charlesgate Hall, we compose uproariously naughty parodies of songs from the Workshop's current musical. We laugh so hard, we can hardly walk straight down Commonwealth Avenue's central boulevard.

When we eat out, after Freddie's paid the waiter we both stand. He goes to retrieve our coats from the rack at the front entrance while I stay put and stretch an arm out to the side, pointing to him. He comes streaking across the floor between us with my coat held open and hooks the proper sleeve on my outstretched arm as he passes me. It's almost as fulfilling as dancing on tables! I'm sure that college students have license to be free, even to astound other diners.

Certainly one needn't be a lady this soon.

Charlesgate Hall, seven stories high, was once a residential hotel for the well-to-do, but it has now been cut up into dormitory rooms clustered in suites. At the corners of the building, the rooms are nestled within high, round turrets which, along with the all-female tenancy, gives the building its nickname: The Witches' Castle. After depositing me safely there, Freddie takes the subway to North Station, where he catches the train to Lynn, the town on the North Shore where he lives with his parents. One Friday afternoon instead of returning me to The Witches' Castle, he takes me home to meet his folks.

The boundary line between two towns runs diagonally through his parents' two-story house. The front door is in Lynn, the back door in Swampscott. I tease Freddie that he needs a passport to go to the bathroom…which, incidentally, I need to visit shortly after we arrive. When I close the door behind me, the room is dark, and I don't detect a light switch. But I perceive that the toilet seat is raised, and I lower it. As it touches the porcelain rim, the light turns on overhead. *Crazy modern inventions!* I think. *But how do the men see what they're doing?*

As I exit, Fred is standing nearby and says, "I turned the light on for you." When he points to the wall switch *outside the room*, I burst out laughing—HA HA not *tee hee*—at my mistake. In Connecticut every light switch is *inside* the room it serves, and even my Boston dormitory doesn't have the silly external placement. But now I know to locate the all-important toggle before I enter any room in and around Beantown.

My boyfriend's family quickly makes me feel at home. His well-padded mother has made a special Sabbath meal, including a luxion coogle baked in a casserole dish. Although I don't appreciate most of my own mother's cooking, this noodle pudding is something she makes exceedingly well, and Mrs. B's can't compare. I learn that she adds crushed pineapple, and I don't favor its intrusion. Every time Freddie brings me home after that, his mom leaves the pineapple out of what she announces is Judy's Corner of the coogle. You can't be much more accepted than that!

Freddie and I are a couple all of our junior year, but by springtime, although my parents have come to visit Roan in Boston, they have not yet met my boyfriend. One weekend, even though my mind is just beginning to whisper so softly that I'm not sure I'm hearing it, "Is it time to move on?" I unwisely bring Freddie B. home to Hebron Street.

Beautiful long, dark lashes fringe his big brown eyes, but his build is slight, and he moves more like Vaslav Nijinsky than Jim Thorpe. Worse, his ambitions lie in the theater, not medicine or finance. My parents just manage a formal greeting and a spattering of polite chatter.

Fred is to sleep that night on the day bed in the sunroom. At dinnertime, the folks appear in that room, Dad unfolds a bridge table in the corner, and Mother sets it with an embroidered linen cloth and fine tableware. Dad opens two bridge chairs as Mother, now full of charm, says, "We thought you'd like a nice, romantic dinner for just the two of you." Although we're puzzled by this strange private repast, the food and service from the kitchen are commendable, and Freddie and I always enjoy being together.

In the morning, Mother serves us a specially prepared breakfast, again at our secluded table, and it seems that we are being royally catered to. After we eat, we thank the folks, pack up, and are about to leave when my father calls my name from behind the closed door of the front bedroom. I go to him, ready for a warm farewell embrace. He's lounging on one of the maple beds, a cigar in the corner of his mouth. He looks up at me with a stony face and with tight lips speaks four words: "Get rid of him."

This edict comes from the daddy who stroked my hair, hid out with me in his basement workshop, fished and did puzzles with me, and gave me my first cigarette. Yet he doesn't know me well enough to understand that his abrupt command has just given Freddie a three-month reprieve. But then, I read my parents so poorly that I've only just realized that the pretty little table for two was due not to romantic sympathies but rather, in spite of their claims of refinement, to a failure of civility. They simply couldn't bring themselves to sit at table with a daughter's guest who repulsed their aristocratic dreams.

THE LADY EMERGES

The Gershwin Workshop's closing-night cast parties are straight out of La Boheme. Boston's Haymarket disbands just about the time our performance ends, and a couple of the guys go down to the open-air stalls with our pooled coins to pick up, for a song, bags of about-to-be-discarded soft fruit along with a selection of unsold cheeses and cheap wine. They bring it all back to where the rest of us wait in a cast member's Beacon Hill rooftop atelier, where the actress/painter turns disfavored canvases upside down to make lap trays for the food. Amid our high-spirited camaraderie and bawdy laughter, no firm fruit or fine wine could be any more delectable.

Entranced, I arrive in Hartford for winter break and announce to my mother that I'm going to change my major from journalism to theater. Without batting an eye or waiting for Dad, she sweetly muses, "Oh, how nice! Now your father and I can be relieved of the expense of your education." I remain a journalism major, but my heart is in the theater.

Then a strange thing happens at a cast party. On a quick trip to our hostess' bathroom, our outrageously good-looking leading man comes across a sheet of instructions that's fallen out of a box of tampons. He returns to the studio, jumps up on a table and—no, he doesn't dance, but he reads the instructions out loud, his lusty asides eliciting raucous responses from the cast. Instead of joining in the general hilarity, I cringe. I squirm. At this point, Mother's carefully trained lady steps forward within me and asks, "What are you doing here?"

I love acting, singing, dancing, directing, and everything about the theater. But all at once my companions and the Bohemian life lose their allure. Since it's a credit class, I continue in the Workshop till the end of the semester, but I place greater emphasis on my writing studies all the way up to receiving my B.S. in journalism, just as my folks have expected. I have almost as many credits in theater, with government taking third place.

This confusing adolescence is the most challenging role of all!

SUMMER IN BOSTON

Journalism professor Reginald Coggeshall is all bear outside and all honey inside. His gruff exterior doesn't fool his students, especially the coeds, who are devoted to him. Getting back articles we've written with a different colored mark slashed across each kind of defection from good journalism is an incisive learning experience we value, and we know he cares about us as people.

For instance, instead of going on vacation, Coggie agrees to teach city editing in the summer of 1952 if I can recruit three other students to take it then. I do, and because I'll be in Boston all summer, I can inherit the coveted paid internship with amiable Al Longo and Sandy Giampapa in the Somerset Hotel publicity office. I gather statistics, write publicity, and once even pose for newspaper photos in my swimsuit, riding a lawnmower we're promoting. How *now*, former fat girl! Late every weekday afternoon, I take the subway from the hotel in Back Bay to downtown and walk a route delivering copy to city editors of four different newspapers.

I get back to the dorm in the most oppressive humidity of the day. Understanding that hot air rises and cool air falls, my two roommates and I remove our outer clothes and sit quietly on the floor in our undies, playing Hearts. By the sound of the cheers and groans from nearby Fenway Park, we can tell the difference between a Red Sox home run and an opponent's brilliant outfield play that robs us of one, and we follow the game by the crowd noise.

Early in the summer, when I'm sure it's my own decision, I sever my relationship with Freddie B. and the theatrical world. In my government class, a fellow in the back row and I notice each other, but his friends warn him that I'm going steady. We get that cleared up during class break when I ask him for a light for my cigarette, and he asks me out. Sam is low-key, fun, and disturbingly sexy. A fervent fan of the Celtics, he takes me often to watch them play in Boston Garden and teaches me the game. Before long I'm crazy about basketball, the Celtics, and Sam.

He lives with his folks in suburban Newton, and one Friday night he, too, takes me home for dinner. But he hasn't forewarned me. As we enter the house, certain strategic lights are lit. Their need has been anticipated, and they've been turned on before sundown. They will not be turned off, and no other light will be added till after sundown Saturday. A picture of my murky old Sabbath school classroom flashes before me.

I don't feel any friendly vibes from Sam's unsmiling father. At the dinner table, after his wife has blessed the candles, he picks up the *challah*, braces it against his body with one hand, and recites the blessing over bread while the other hand slices it toward his chest with a knife surely descended from a saber. I try not to look bug-eyed.

Chulnt is served for dinner. The stew of beef, lima beans, potatoes, and barley prepared Friday afternoon simmers on a very low flame all day Saturday, so that it's always ready to be served without lighting a burner. I haven't tasted *chulnt* since visiting Uncle Morris and Big Aunt Rose in childhood. Didn't like it then and don't like it now.

But it's yet another visit to a bathroom that ends my summer romance. In Sam's house I discover that the toilet tissue has already been torn into measured portions before sundown to preclude that work on the Sabbath. I have never encountered this before. I mean to respect every family's culture, but this one is a real challenge. Suddenly Sam is not so sexy.

Venturing

A PLACE OF MY OWN

At last, after holding my breath since the age of fifteen, in October of 1952 I reach my legal majority. At twenty-one, I can finally direct my own life without fear of being dragged "home."

In early December, joyfully immersed in the essence of historic Boston, I walk along Beacon Street's red brick sidewalk checking out little Apartment for Let signs in the windows of dowager brownstones. I alert my friends that I'm looking for a roommate and am introduced to the daughter of a millionaire from Newton, who aims to be a perpetual urban student. ("Roomie," she later laughs, "You know I'll never work.") I find a fourth-floor walkup at the back of a converted ancient brownstone that will cost us each nine dollars a week starting in January. Toni agrees to the deal sight unseen, and in exchange for a deposit, the landlord gives me the key.

In the square sitting room, a large fireplace shares wall space with windows that overlook classy Newbury Street. The entire expanse over the mantel is mirrored, seeming to enlarge the room. The trundle bed against the wall will accommodate each of us separately, and in the morning, when Toni's part is collapsed and rolled under mine, the prominent round, glass-topped cocktail table can be returned to its place in front of the fire.

Off this room, the walk-in closet/dressing room is

actually bigger than the kitchen alcove scraped out of a more meager closet. The miniscule kitchen accommodates a basic stove, refrigerator, sink, and a bridge table in the corner on which to both prepare and eat our meals, in the absence of counter space. The linoleum just under the table and two bridge chairs is thin and dingy; the rest of the floor consists of bare wooden slats. A tiny bathroom off the kitchen has two doors—one from our apartment and another from that of two young gentlemen up front. Since there's no lock on either door, all four of us will unfailingly knock before entering. When inside we'll loudly whistle or sing. Showers will be hurried, nervous musicals. Yet the system will work so well that on the day Toni and I move out, we will not even know what the other fourth floor tenants look like. We'll have managed not to bump into them in the hall and will know them only by ear.

Winter break from school is the culmination of my past six years' cherished dreams. Though officially an adult now, I am so immersed in my struggle to emerge that I don't consider the shock to my parents' own dreams after assuring me an educated shot at a fulfilling future. I wave the key to the apartment before them and announce that I'm not coming home when I finish school in January.

I see my mother's eyes turn from liquid brown to grey steel. Every line in her face hardens and its roundness seems to rush to a sharp point. She proclaims, "There's only *one* reason a girl takes an apartment out of town."

I retort, "If that's what you can think of me, then that's what you deserve to think. I will not stoop to defend myself."

The exchange is in line with our habit of verbally slugging it out rather than harboring our anger. Because fury doesn't fester secretly within us, Mother and I are able to repair our relationship sooner. It is loud and messy, but when I watch a friend who's been paralyzed by venomous bites of stored-up anger slithering around inside, repeatedly striking without an outlet, I learn to be grateful for our familial catharsis.

So Mother soon softens and clarifies, "I always thought you would stay safely under my wing until you were safely married." Poor Mother, that's why I have a key to an apartment in Boston.

A FULL TIME JOB

Back in Boston, I make the rounds of employment agencies. Though I want to write for a living, I don't share Mother's conflicted, romantic vision of me as a glamorous girl reporter (safely under her wing). I recoil from the thought of asking the parents of a rape or murder victim the inane "How do you feel?" I simply couldn't request a picture of their daughter to plaster all over our pages while substituting a euphemism for "rape" because the daily newspaper is considered a family medium. As for gossip, I do not believe the public has a right to know private things.

I enjoy creating informative publicity, but there aren't many openings in that field. I'm prepared to start at the bottom, say as a receptionist or stenographer and work my way up. As suggested in their catalogue, I learned shorthand for taking interviews the summer before entering B.U,. and I can take dictation at over one hundred and twenty words per minute. But that becomes unnecessary when, incredibly, I'm hired by a downtown advertising agency as a full-fledged copywriter! One day in January I will attend my last class in the morning and report to work after lunch. I will make forty-two dollars a week. I have never taken a course in advertising, but I know how to write.

Erupting like popcorn in a popper with the incredible news, I call my folks to share my good fortune. I have a job in my field, and I'm on my way! My mother answers the phone. She does not say Congratulations. My mother says, "What will you be paid?" I tell her, and I can hear her sag. She sighs, "For this I sent you to four years of college?"

In the back room of the small ad agency sit Gloria, the bookkeeper, and Ray, a nimble artist who doesn't flinch when I ask him to draw me a crying washing machine. He's been going with a woman for years but has never had the courage to propose marriage. One day there is great excitement in the agency as he announces that he has given his woman an engagement ring. Although he still doesn't sound too sure, and no wedding date has been set, we're all happy for him. The back room pair of Gloria and Ray are pleasant to work with.

When I cash my first paycheck, Gloria teaches me to immediately deposit an amount off the top into a savings account. Then I hand my nine-dollar rent to our landlord. I wash out a series of clear food bottles, apportion among them my remaining cash slated for food, shopping, and entertainment, and line them up on the high shelf in the kitchen. If I want to attend a play or concert, I turn over the Fun bottle to see if I can afford it. This is my budget. No one lures me into fiscal trouble by offering credit, and my monetary condition is literally transparent.

Gloria lives in a modestly appointed apartment at the foot of Beacon Hill, and on a Friday night we may usher in the weekend by having dinner together at either her place or mine. (Toni is rarely home.) More often we take advantage of happy hour in one of the attractive cocktail lounges that offer free hors d'oeuvre buffets with one-dollar drinks. We make a whole meal of tasty hot meatballs, cocktail franks, cheeses, crackers and crudités for the price of a single martini. Sometimes we retire right afterward to our separate apartments, others we see a great British comedy at the movie theater on Exeter Street. It's an easy walk for both of us, and the streets are safe at night.

So safe that I think nothing of taking the subway by

myself to a movie or play downtown or even alertly walking home alone across the Common after dark. (After seeing the Hans Christian Andersen film, I can't help dancing half way home to the music still in my head until I note a poor homeless fellow trying to sleep on a park bench and quiet down.) If I take the subway and there's a rare drunk on the platform, I just make sure to stand unobtrusively at a distance till the train comes. The best way to hurry the train is to light a Dunhill; then it appears so fast that the cigarette is wasted. It always works, and I arrive home safely under my own wing.

Over time I learn to play a little game with my ad agency boss, Henry. He buys one minute of radio time and assigns me to write a one-minute spot. I submit for his approval exactly one minute of copy. He picks up his pencil before even starting to read, and when he's done there's a minute-and-a-half's worth of words on the page. I go to my desk and retype the commercial with his additions. The time salesman from the radio station comes to pick it up, and Henry hands it to him, Hack says it's too long, and in front of him, Henry instructs me to cut it down. Again I retype the spot, cutting out some of my words to fit in some of Henry's, and the rep takes it back to the station for airing. This happens so regularly that I begin saving the original of my first effort. Hack is onto the game. When he leaves Henry's office with the greedy version trying to cram in one-and-a-half minutes' worth of advertising while only paying for one, he comes to my desk, swaps that version for my original, we exchange a secret smile, and he goes on his way. This saves everyone wasted effort except Henry. He hasn't time to listen to every commercial as broadcast and never knows that his words haven't hit the air. The client says the ad is bringing him business, and we're all happy. Except for my still, small voice.

It's an ill wind that blows no good—Henry's shenanigans elevate my bowling average! Boston alleys set up a triangle of ten candle pins, taller and with a slight swell in the middle instead of the bottom bulge of Hartford's duck pins. Deadwood is left where it falls, and the deft bowler can aim the next ball at it and spin the deadwood to knock down widely spaced standing pins. The bowler still uses three small, light balls sans finger hole per turn, unless she needs only one or two for a strike or spare. Now I up my average with a new technique: I picture Henry's face between the #1 and #3 pins, let the ball rip, and score many more marks!

One day he comes back from a lunch meeting with an appliance retailer and hands me a napkin on which is written "The Hallman Plan." He says, "Write me three one-minute spots on this."

"Okay, what is the Hallman Plan?"

"I don't know, and you don't need to know," he tells me.

I suspect there is no Hallman Plan, but I write three one-minute spots that make money for Hallman, Henry, and Hack. This is not the kind of writing I've dreamed of doing.

Yet I have to admit that Monday mornings are fun. I phone up the stock car race promoter and ask who won the Sunday races and if there were any crashes, collisions, near misses, or other notable events. With that information, I write a bird's-eye review of the day's activity for the evening paper. After I invent daredevil nicknames for the drivers and enliven the facts without distorting their truth, I dare you to suspect that not only was I not in the stands, but that I have never been to a car race.

The things that save my soul are the elegant, classical print ads I create for the designer of church interiors. I'm proud when I see them on the glossy pages of *Architectural Digest* or my chic ads for ladies' clothes in *Women's Wear Daily*. Otherwise, I'm beginning not to like the business of advertising or myself.

SIP OR SWIG

Life's embarrassing moments: In 1953 I was dating Bob, a fellow from Toni's millionaire crowd. When he invited me to a dinner his parents were giving, I was somewhat nervous but dressed carefully, and confident of my upbringing, I felt I could hold my own.

As the guests assembled in the living room before dinner, I was sitting on the bench before the grand piano. When drinks were offered around by a uniformed server, Bob took two small cordial glasses off the tray and passed one to me.

The only time I'd seen a liquor glass that small, it didn't have a stem, and it contained the schnapps my parents served at holidays. I'd seen my father and his friends knock it back in one gulp, and feeling so sophisticated, I did likewise with the drink Bob handed me. As I lowered my head and the empty glass, it seemed that every startled eye in the room was trained on me.

Uh-oh. Bob answered my questioning look with the whispered information, "You're supposed to sip it slowly." Oh. I'd never heard of an aperitif that was to be sipped slowly and never seen the delicate stemware it was served in. I felt like Eliza Doolittle. Always after that, whether we were in company or alone, when drinks were served, I'd quietly ask Bob out of the side of my mouth: sip or swig?

Like my friend Nortie who decreed that a girl had to

play bridge and tennis to be socially acceptable, Toni insisted that if I was going to travel in Bob's crowd I must drink Scotch. I tried. I really did, and I was able to fake it for a while. But as soon as I stopped dating Bob, I jettisoned Scotch whiskey. The stuff is really vile.

I was naïve about alcohol because I hadn't been interested in it since my cousin Berry's bar mitzvah. At the reception Cousin Murray, then a wiseacre of no more than thirteen himself, repeatedly hit the spiked punch bowl when no one was looking and ended up not feeling so well. Since he was from out of town, my parents brought him back to our Blue Hills Avenue flat to lie down on the daybed in our playroom. In short order Murray splattered his entire bar mitzvah lunch onto the wall next to the bed. UGH! Mother, with the help of the maid who occupied that bed nightly, rushed to clean up the mess. But a dark stain marked that wallpaper as long as we lived in the flat. Younger than my cousins by several years, every time I walked into that room, revulsion hit me. For a long time I had no interest in anything that could produce such a yucky result.

Before I went off to college, Dad tried to educate me in ladylike libation. He would offer me a drink when making them for company, but imagining the sweetness that a combination of Coca Cola and rum must be, my face screwed up and my head shook no even without my volition. Eventually Dad gave up and just warned me never to mix proofs. I listened gratefully and have never been drunk— only overcome by giggles on a couple of fun occasions. I'm not unhappy to have missed the full range of possibilities.

My first official cocktail was a Tom Collins. Traditionally, at the dinner ending the Phi Sigma Sigma pledge period, each mentoring sorority "mother" would buy her freshman "daughter" a drink. I didn't want to deny my sponsor this tradition and asked her what was the mildest thing I could order. Sandy introduced me to Tom, and that was my drink until...

Technically, UConn was a dry campus, but on Saturday nights the fraternity houses drew their drapes and served alcohol at their parties. Sure was miraculous that neither the house mothers, the administration, nor those heroes who ferreted out illicit hotplates got even a whiff of it! At those parties I nursed one Tom Collins all evening. Until I spotted Randy.

He was working off his fraternity dues by, among other duties, serving as bartender at Phi Sigma Delta parties. Gosh, he was appealing! I wanted him to ask me out, but since he had little money and I was always with another date, I figured I had to send a subtle message that it wouldn't be burdensome.

I knew that beer costs less than mixed drinks. All the girls screwed up their noses at the taste, but I convinced a sorority sister that we should teach ourselves to drink it. We hitched into Willi and after a movie went next door to the package store, which didn't ask for I.D.

"Two Schlitz," I ordered.

"Two WHAT of Schlitz?" the clerk demanded. I panicked to think he knew we were under age, but he took our money when I specified two cold cans of the stuff. Then, in case we absolutely hated it, we went to a grocery and bought a pint of ice cream to eradicate the taste.

After an uneventful ride back to campus, we pulled the shades in my room, sat on my bed and slowly sipped our brew, by now lukewarm. I grimaced along with my friend at the first swallow, but by the bottom of the can, I found I *liked* it. Even so, when we'd each slowly emptied our beer, we polished off our dessert. All my life since, I've retained a taste for warm beer with slightly melted ice cream.

Well, back in '51 my devious plan worked. When I began asking for beer instead of Tom Collins at Phi Sig Delta parties, Randy noticed and indeed asked me out. We dated pleasantly, inexpensively, and briefly. But he wasn't The One and was forgotten when I went to Boston. There the *de rigeuer* drink was gin and tonic. I fit in fine. I liked the gardenia smell of gin and enjoyed an occasional martini— stirred, not shaken.

There was a little café around the corner from Charlesgate Hall where the coeds sometimes liked to have Sunday breakfast. In obedience to Boston's Blue Laws, if we'd even wanted an alcoholic drink before noon, it could not have been ordered at the bar, only at our booth. What we heathens did want was some music with breakfast. Uh uh. If we put a nickel in the table-side jukebox before noon, when the State of Massachusetts thought we should be in church, it wouldn't work.

The host at my favorite date venue greeted patrons with "Welcome to the Ba-**VAAA**-rian Rathskeller!" Singing waiters in lederhosen and frauleins in flouncy skirts served German beer in thirty-two-ounce glass steins. During the evening a suspendered musical conductor pulled down a movie screen and pointed his baton to projected objects and their German names while patrons sang Schnitzelbank to the accompaniment of an oompah band. What fun when the conductor pointed to the picture of the sour old mother-in-law, asked *Ist das nicht ein schveigermutter?* and we answered in unison, *Ja, das ist ein schveigermutter* and sang the refrain, *Ei du schoeneh, schnitzelbank.* It was at the Bavarian Rathskeller that I fell in love with dark, full-bodied beers, which are a whole different animal from a can of Schlitz. They are never served in delicate little glasses with stems, and I don't drink them with ice cream.

THE GREAT NON-EVENT

I've already been working for six months when I receive my B.S. in journalism in June 1953. It happens on the Celtics basketball court in Boston Garden. Joining the crowd of graduates in the arena, I'm surprised and excited to be hugged in welcome by classmates I haven't seen since January. Some people who finished classes early aren't bothering with the ceremony, but I want to feel the swell of pride walking down the aisle to the regal music of Pomp and Circumstance (which activates my tear ducts no matter who's marching), wearing the white cap and gown that confirm my achievement. I've made Dean's List my last seven semesters. I have earned this celebration, and I want to present it as a gift to my parents, who made it possible.

I'm able to spot them in the huge complex housed in North Station by hearing my father's distinctive throat-clearing and recognizing my mother's hat. I look directly up at them to make a connection in the moment before I'm handed my diploma. Neither one of them is looking at me. Neither one is smiling. Is it too late for them to be proud of me? Of themselves?

When the program's over, we meet outside and Dad drives Mother and me straight to my apartment. Roan is back in Hartford tending her four children. In the car my parents query whether I have a romantic interest and are unhappy when I say no. Coeds only half joke that their parents send them to school to meet a smart college boy full of potential and earn their M.R.S. I have failed. I am living in my own apartment and making forty-six dollars a week (after a ten percent raise) instead of being safely married and making babies.

My father inquires—INQUIRES!—if I'd like them to take me out to lunch. Nothing has been previously planned. But the air is ponderous with their desire to start the two-hour drive back to Hartford before the day gets late. Though my roommate hasn't acknowledged my graduation in any way, I let my parents off the hook by fibbing that she's arranged a celebration in the apartment later. They express no interest in seeing my living quarters, viewing the party decorations, or meeting my roommate. They don't even need a pit stop. Okay then, they say, and after we take a few snapshots on the sidewalk (without the rented cap and gown), they drive off.

So! That is the glorious climax to my four years of college. I climb the stairs alone to my fourth-floor walk-up. Inside the empty apartment I crumple onto the trundle bed and open the floodgates to the sobs of hurt and disappointment that I've been holding at bay.

After a while I remember that Toni's friend Harry has told me if I ever need anything to call him. I dial his number and through my tears ask if he'll take me to dinner to mark my commencement. He does one better—in a lovely restaurant he talks my tears away while he wines and dines me, and afterward we sit necking in his car. We both understand that we'll never date, but Harry's generous offering of a little gentle love is what I need to survive the awful emptiness of this day.

GOING FORWARD

Toni has become involved with a visiting director from the Abbey Theater who has a wife and children back in Ireland. I'm alone in the apartment more and more, and when she's there I don't want to hear of their escapades. Fortunately, she abides by our original agreement not to bring members of the opposite sex back to our shared space. The music store around the corner has a standing order to notify Toni as soon as a new classical record comes in. With her unlimited allowance, she runs right down and buys it, and there are some pleasant times when the two of us just sit and listen to exquisite music. But too often the poignancy of those works stirs up my unutterable loneliness.

One weekend I'm attacked by a virus that makes it hurt like hell when anything touches my skin. It's not unusual for Toni to sleep elsewhere, and I'm by myself, awake well into the night, sitting bolt upright in the trundle bed without either nightclothes or covers. I'm reading Philip Wylie's clever book, The Disappearance, by the light of a small lamp when I hear a door softly open. I realize that someone has entered our kitchen through the bathroom. I quickly wrap myself in my emergency blanket and call out. Our landlord appears, holding an apple, which he has just filched from our refrigerator. He says he didn't see a light and thought nobody was home. Out of stark fear and the pain of the blanket on my skin, from my vulnerable position I unleash a storm of invective to outclass Mother. The landlord makes a hasty retreat. I check my budget bottles and find no money gone, but before the week is out, I've moved with Toni to an apartment on Commonwealth Avenue. It has a secure lock, a discrete bedroom with bunk beds, a living room, kitchen, private bathroom…and, we soon learn, cockroaches in the apartment across the hall.

Roaches are not unusual in the old houses in Back Bay. I've never been squeamish about bugs, but cockroaches are bigger and even more revolting than the Japanese beetles I used to pick off the Zaccagninos' grapevines. Besides, they move like lightning! Fortunately, none visit our own apartment, but when our young neighbor living alone spots one in her place, she screams. I pick up a shoe or book and go to her. She points to the intruder, I calculate the windage and unleash my weapon just in time to vanquish the speeding target. I never dreamed I'd embark upon a second career as the fastest roach slayer on Commonwealth Avenue!

Otherwise, Boston has lived up to my dreams, and I love being on my own in this city. I'm thrilled to take money from my entertainment jar and buy a ticket to hear the eminent Joseph Szigeti play violin in nearby Jordan Hall. I'm enchanted by the Italianate architecture, hanging flowers, tapestried furniture and paintings of the Isabella Stewart Gardner Museum. I gleefully root for the Red Sox and the Celtics. Boston's restaurants are superb. Yet, though Schrafft's coffee shop serves a heavenly hot fudge sundae in a pool of deep green mint sauce topped by whipped cream and a cherry, I still wear a size seven dress.

Only, although I have lots of dates, I'm not meeting the kind of friends or boyfriends I'd like. To position oneself to meet nice Jewish boys, a girl is advised to join the Beth Israel Hospital Auxiliary, make friends and be introduced to the girls' brothers, cousins, and male acquaintances. But when I attend a meeting, the young socialite members huddle in such an unbelievably self-absorbed, impenetrable clique that not one even looks up to acknowledge a new face, let alone welcome her. If that's how these ladies were brought up, I don't think I want to meet their brothers or cousins. I'm in the wrong place again, and I never return.

Toni now trades the Irish director for a contemporary theater classmate. They enjoy drinking together, though abiding by our rooming agreement, not in the apartment. I'm to call friend Harry if she ever comes home drunk because I've warned her I won't take care of her. She's tested me just once and seen me hang up and head for the movies without waiting for Harry to arrive.

I've quickly received a raise at work, and in spite of her daddy's riches, Toni periodically asks me for a short-term loan to buy Boyfriend martinis. She knows I'll refuse. I'd really like to chuck her, but I still need her half of the rent. At least that's always on time.

I've selected the upper level of our bunk bed for the greatest privacy. One day I come home from work and find Toni has broken our pact; there's a half-clothed man in my bed. She explains from the lower level that he is her boyfriend's older brother. He's on a short R&R from the church he leads, which he claims the clergy traditionally uses to drink and play cards. But in spite of his placement in the upper bunk at the moment, it's obviously not cards they've been playing.

It's hard enough after the Kinsey Report has come out to be a normal, healthy but firmly raised young lady, still guarding her virginity like the Crown Jewels, without rooming with a woman who lives by different standards. I instantly march out of the apartment with the demand that Father Brother be gone when I return, and that week I respond to an ad for a roommate to share a *3½ rm. apt. on the Fenway.* After Florence Perlman and I conduct a mutually careful interview, I move in.

My new home is in a modern apartment house, not a converted brownstone. Behind a locked door Florence and I have a bedroom with two single beds, a bathroom, living room, full kitchen, and even a separate dinette with a real dining table. There are no cockroaches and no screamers in the building. Our second-floor apartment can even be reached by elevator. Just a block away is Symphony Hall, where I attend free dress rehearsals of the magnificent Boston Symphony Orchestra under world-renowned conductors. A big bonus is being able to talk and listen to my roommate without embarrassment.

I wouldn't give up one day of learning that I can survive in a challenging milieu, but with a more compatible roommate, my piercing loneliness mercifully eases. Although Florence is a night-shift nurse at the hospital and I work during the day, our time, especially on weekends, overlaps enough to become friends. She even takes me to Salem to meet her widowed mother and her kid sister, and we get along like family.

My own family has not returned to Boston since my graduation. They have never seen where I live. When Roan and Howard were first married, they lived frugally in economy apartments first in Back Bay, then Medford, and finally in Somerville. By the time they moved back to the Hartford area and bought their own home, they had two children, with twins on the way. My parents were happy to be unburdened of a two-hour drive to visit their good daughter and their grandbabies. Meanwhile, since I'm still rummaging around for myself in that amorphous mess inside the redhead in the mirror, I guess there's no incentive to make the long drive just to see their "quirky kid." That appellation has replaced *vilda chaya* as Mother's favorite epithet for me. How many times do I hear, "You always were a quirky kid." Was I? Am I?

In spite of the name-calling, I begin to wonder about returning to my roots. I need someone to love for a lifetime. Now that I've progressed from the school, theater, and millionaire scenes, I'm happier with the fellows I meet, but I begin to see the benefit of a backdrop of family and community. My father has never stopped urging me to come back, and in April 1954, with no small trepidation—theirs and mine—I return to my parents' home.

TO MARKET, TO MARKET

As soon as I'm home, Mother's friend Sadie gives my phone number to a nice single Jewish fellow she knows. We hit it off and see each other all summer. Guess what? He and his friends are avid bridge players! They spend more time at the beach playing cards on the blanket than swimming in the ocean. I learn the game and am now almost there on the social acceptability scale, although I find reading, swimming, and conversing more rewarding. Nevertheless, Dean and I do well as bridge partners, he's pleased with me, and I like his circle of friends.

Further networking, Little Aunt Rose has a connection in radio advertising and gets me an appointment to be interviewed. The man has me cooling my heels in the waiting room of his agency for almost forty-five minutes before summoning me into his inner sanctum without apology. He barely glances at my resume and portfolio before launching into an incoherent lecture.

"Nobody gets special treatment here," he growls. "Advertising is a dog-eat-dog business, and there are too many predators out there." Whoa! Was this brought on by overly energetic efforts on my behalf by Aunt Rose, or is this guy just a jerk? I make no attempt to charm the boor but remain polite out of respect to my aunt. The interview ends quickly by tacit mutual agreement. Were this guy to offer me a job, I wouldn't touch it with a ten-foot pole. I remember that I wanted to get out of the business anyway.

Hartford being the insurance capital of the world, I run straight from Mr. Advertising to the home office of Hartford Accident & Indemnity Co. There I'm immediately hired as secretary to Lyn Brown, Jr. in the Fidelity and Surety Bond Salvage Department. Once a claim is paid, our responsibility is to make contact with the embezzler or defaulting contractor who caused the loss and recover our money.

I like and respect Lyn Brown. I respect The Hartford, and I find my job fascinating. In six months I'm promoted to Junior Claim Examiner and handle my own cases. Working with the claim examiners in our branch offices across the country, I'm part skip tracer, part lawyer, and part parole officer, convincing folks to straighten out their lives and stick to a plan of reimbursement. A far cry from journalism, but I love it!

I'm heading toward twenty-three years old and already a spinster in my mother's eyes. It's true, two years after graduating college there aren't many single girls left in Hartford. But my brother-in-law Howard has a likeable cousin my age with whom I become friends. Carol and I resist our mothers' urgings to hunt husbands in the resorts of New York's Catskill Mountains, generally known as a "meet market." I tell Mother that the kind of man I'm waiting for isn't going to the Catskills shopping for me, and I stand my ground.

My recent roommate Florence calls from Boston and suggests we go to Nantucket for the weekend. I've never been to that historic whaling island, and it sounds like a great break! I take the train to Boston, where Florence meets me and brings me to Salem to spend the night with her mom and sister.

The next morning at Logan Airport, I recall that when I was a small girl, our folks took Roan and me to Rentschler Airport in East Hartford to treat my big sister to a private airplane ride. When everything was ready, Roan started forward but was suddenly seized with dread and changed her mind. Dad tried to allay her fears and encourage her onto the plane, but she was too spooked and started back toward the car. Hopping up and down, I begged, "Take me! Take me!" but as usual, I was too young or too small or too something. Neither Roan nor I boarded the aircraft that day, and it became another thing I determined to do when I ran my own life.

Now walking across the tarmac toward the plane to Nantucket, I can hardly contain myself. As I start up the stairs to the cabin, my heart is giddily singing, "I'm really here! I'm doing it! I'm actually going to fly!" And I don't need anyone's permission.

I love it when the plane picks up speed hurtling down the runway. I love the little jolt when its wheels leave the ground and we become airborne. I love the short hop across Nantucket Sound, over too quickly. But at my first sight of the hotel from our island taxi, my euphoria brakes to a sudden halt. I've been anticipating a charming, historic, salt-smelling haven. Instead it's a busy meet market! Since there's not just heavy fog but drizzle outside, the damp, noisy hotel lobby is full of singles milling around trying to meet each other. So this is what Florence had in mind!

Well, I'm not going to waste this island. After we settle in our room, I return to the lobby with my friend just long enough for her to get oriented. I'm wearing a floral-printed dress with a softly flared, knee-length skirt and a simple bow at the neckline. All the other girls are clad in the new popular Bermuda shorts with casual tops. A pair of them sitting on a window ledge tell me I must go right out to one of the nearby shops and outfit myself in similar uniform.

Don't be so serious, my sorority sisters tell me, and don't be so dramatic!

Don't laugh ha-ha, *Aunt Rose says.*

*Must play bridge, Nortie tells me in the cafeteria line,
and must play tennis.*
Must drink Scotch, Toni advises.
*Don't be disrespectful, Dad says, and must be a lady,
Mother insists.*
Now, must get Bermuda shorts.
*Stop! With so many Don't Be's and Must Be's
swirling round me, is there nothing I Am that's acceptable?
The cacophony makes it hard to figure out Who I Want to Be.*
But right now I know what I came here for.

"No," I firmly tell the girls in the hotel lobby, "I'm
not going shopping; I'm going beach-combing."

"In the drizzle?"

"Oh, yes, even better in the drizzle."

A nice-looking fellow overhears me and comes over
to drape his raincoat over my shoulders. "You can return it
later," he says. The Misses Bermuda Shorts glare.

I walk down to the waterfront and sit on a wooden
bench for a long, peaceful time watching the stillness of a
sailboat whose upper mast is lost in the fog. The mob in the
lobby fades from memory as I inhale the calm, and soon the
drizzle stops.

After a while I stroll among the streets, admiring the
quaint shops and the Colonial homes topped with square,
white-railed widow's walks. I can almost see a whaler's wife
pacing up there, her eyes searching the sea for the return of
her husband's ship. The gardens of homes and shops are
bursting with colorful, rain-nourished blooms. I walk down
grey weathered piers lined with craft studios, art galleries,
and small shops full of fishing gear. I board a tour bus that
circles the picturesque island, and I see how the climate
produces an eye-popping profusion of glorious roses.

Back at my starting point, I walk over to the nearby
beach, remove my shoes, and let the wet sand squish
between my bare toes while, as when I was a child, I collect
luminescent pink-orange pearl shells. Late in the day I go

back to the hotel with my borrowed coat's pockets full of those shells and other intriguing finds. I empty and brush out the pockets and return the coat with thanks. Since the owner was successful in making a connection while I was gone, we have no further discourse.

Other seekers are still seeking, but now that the rain has let up, they're mingling in the street. The indignity of it all touches me with sadness. Florence spots me and comes to convey that there's to be a party on the island that night but nobody has yet paired off. A group is about to go over to another beach on rented bicycles, and a guy near me asks if I'd like to ride on his handle bars. I accept, and the trip is fun, but once there, toasting marshmallows is just another form of milling around. Back at the hotel, I fall into conversation with a different fellow and am startled when he asks me to go to dinner and the party with him.

Oh, my.

I say only if he has a date for my roommate. *After all, she's been working on this all day.* He does have a friend, so we make up a foursome.

I allow myself a silent triumphant laugh at the expense of my would-be fashion consultants when, during the evening, Alvin tells me, "You know, I asked you out because you're the only girl on Nantucket wearing a dress and looking like a girl." Yet I turn out to be a disappointment. All goes well at dinner; but at the party we form teams to play Botticelli, sort of an oral crossword puzzle. After I've come up with several answers for our team, my date looks at his friends with embarrassment and says, "Honestly, she didn't sound like this when I asked her out." Now I have the picture: wear dress, keep brain hidden. Later I have another surprise for him: forget about the goodnight kiss you're seeking from the girl who needs to be apologized for.

Believe it or not, after returning to Connecticut, Alvin calls and asks me out again. I can't imagine why I accept—out of curiosity, I guess. But after a day of swimming at a Stamford beach, I get in trouble again at dinner in the nearby home of his sister and brother-in-law. Adlai Stevenson is running for president against Dwight Eisenhower, and I comment that Stevenson's stance on unilateral disarmament frightens me. This leads to a thoughtful discussion with the relatives...but not with Alvin. I look at his stolid face, and we both know there won't be another date. I'm not sorry.

Well, at least I can say I went to market and met.

HOME AGAIN, HOME AGAIN, JIGGITY JIG

At first Mother, Dad, and I lived together in a surprising state of tolerance and relative peace. I was comfortable in the front bedroom with the maple double beds and pretty flowered wallpaper. The daily enjoyment of my position at The Hartford and going out with Dean on weekends produced some welcome stasis in me. I didn't seem to upset the folks too much except for still being stubbornly single.

Then just before Rosh Hashannah in the fall, watching me hunt through my closet for something appropriate to wear to synagogue, my father suddenly boiled over. His sneer, "You *never* have the right clothes!" jolted me. I was heartsick. I had done this. I had so disappointed my old loving buddy that I had turned his light-hearted badinage into a heartbreaking snarl.

I wasn't nearly so affected when Mother, incensed over something or other I did or failed to do, rose on her toes and slashed her clenched fists down through the air from her head to her hips, crying out, "WHY DID I BORN YOU?" Mother and I went back such a long way as adversaries that I simply noted with interest that she looked like a rearing horse and used bad grammar. I knew this moment would pass.

There came a day when the two of them returned to Hebron Street after a day out, glowing with elation. They'd just finally bought their own spanking new home in West Hartford! It was a model home, fully carpeted and painted a warm pink inside, and the sale even included its decorator furnishings. I understood what it could mean to them after clearing their Depression debts and putting their daughters through a total of six years of college, I brimmed with happiness for them. It didn't occur to me how much more they could savor it if they moved in alone.

Going with them to the suburbs before I'd learned to drive presented a problem. Bus runs from Hartford to West Hartford were spaced wide apart in the evening. Every Tuesday at 4:15 closing time, a group of us from The Hartford's Girls' Club walked down Asylum Avenue, ate supper at the Capitol Grill, and then continued on to the bowling alley on Asylum Street for league play. I enjoyed being with the girls and loved everything about bowling— the constant rousing clatter of the pins and penciling in strikes and spares on the big score sheet. I laughed at the sight of the pin boy's legs disappearing back up into his hidden lair above the lane after he'd cleared away deadwood or reset the triangle of pins and rolled the three small balls back up the gutter. Often his efforts were accompanied by a mischievous smile and a congratulatory or sympathetic wisecrack. I was always happy to drop some money in the pin boys' tip bottle on the way out of the alley.

When my league finished our three games, it would be dark, and the nighttime bus schedule would be in force. I'd walk alone the block over to the bus stop and stand among a few silent strangers waiting for the suburban carrier to come. In winter I shuffled my feet, paced back and forth, or huddled against the office building behind us, trying to keep my cold-bitten toes alive. The ride to my parents' new neighborhood was long and I still had a cold walk from the bus stop to the house before I could kick off my shoes and wrap my grateful feet in a warming blanket.

One Tuesday night I came home to a house empty

and dark except for one light. In the kitchen I found a note from my father—another biting snarl:

"Since you didn't see fit to let us know you wouldn't be home for supper, we finally ate without you. Your plate is in the refrigerator."

Outrage ignited within me at the injustice of the accusation. Then followed sad recognition that I was such a footnote to their lives that neither could remember where I *always* was on Tuesdays. I was used to Mother's unreliability, but why hadn't Dad reminded her where I was? And if he, too, expected me home, why had they together chosen condemnation over concern? That was the moment when I finally admitted to myself that my father would never be the prince to rescue me.

Furious tears sprouted as I stormed up the stairs to my bedroom. How could I get back at him? I remembered that we had made a pact three days before to stop smoking cigarettes. Both of us had been doing well and were proud of ourselves and each other. I hadn't been carrying any with me, even to the alley where smoking went hand in hand with bowling, laying the cigarette down just long enough to roll the ball. Now I yanked open my bureau drawer and took out the pack I'd put out of sight to avoid temptation. I pulled out one of those deadly white cylinders, lit a spiteful match to it, and inhaled deeply. When my parents got home, I told my father what I'd done.

"I won't keep faith with you if you can't keep faith with me," I said. "Why couldn't you have remembered? Why couldn't you have told her that I eat out and bowl on Tuesdays? Don't you both know that she never cooks for me on Tuesdays?"

His answer: "You will respect your mother. You will call her every Tuesday before you leave work and tell her that you won't be home for dinner." The ball was to be in my court? Oh, no, Father.

I rejoined, "I will respect her when she respects me,"

and we glared at each other.

But they didn't kick me out. The next morning Dad drove me to work, and although constrained, life continued as if nothing had happened. Though I never called my mother from work on Tuesday, she remembered not to make dinner for me. But something had been broken, and my father and I both returned to smoking. He never tried to quit again, and it took me another eight years to conquer the habit. It took sixty more years before I understood how memory slips over a lifetime.

I wish I had known it then.

Taking the Right Turn

MEETING SEYMOUR

My relationship with Dean leading nowhere, I break it off after Labor Day. The game of bridge joins Scotch whiskey in the Discards bin.

I'm starting to entertain the possibility that I may remain an old maid after all, as Mother fears. I envision spending my years traveling the world with tour groups, which could be an exciting and rewarding life—better than being married to the wrong man, I think.

In October my friend Carol asks if I'll go with her to a singles dance at Temple Beth Israel. As much as I hate playing Seek and Find, I like Carol, and since I know she won't go without me, I accompany her. Surprisingly, as I dance in the temple social hall with some new fellows, I don't feel like a commodity. I actually enjoy myself.

The next night I get a phone call. "You don't know me," an agreeable voice says. "My name is Seymour Fenster. I noticed you dancing at the temple last night when Miles Weber was standing next to me. I asked him if he knows you, and he told me your name and what street you live on, so I looked up the phone number." Miles, a good friend of Dean's, understands that it's over between us. Frankly, I'm rather disappointed that he hasn't called me for a date himself, and I wonder how he knows where I live.

Seymour Fenster and I slip easily into conversation. After we've talked for a short time, he asks to take me to dinner the next night. I'm so comfortable with him that I feel no need to play hard-to-get, and I accept. We continue talking. After a while, he suddenly says, "I know I asked you out for tomorrow, but you sound so nice, I can't wait to meet you. May I come over and just talk with you a little tonight?" Though I'm taking my driver's license test tomorrow morning and have planned to review the manual tonight, Seymour's so pleasant that I find myself agreeing. I give him directions to my folks' split-level home.

When the bell rings, Mother answers the door on the main floor and ushers Seymour down the half-flight of stairs to the recreation room, where she and Dad start chatting with him.

In my bedroom on the upper level, I'm having second thoughts. *Blind dates may sound nice on the phone, but you ought to know by now that they mostly turn out to be freaks.*

Steeling myself to be polite to a disappointing guy, I descend the short flight of stairs to the living room. I turn the corner and from the hidden top step of the next half-flight into the rec room, I get a glimpse of this Seymour before he can see me and my surprise. It can't be! He's *adorable!* A calm, smiling face topped by a mass of tight blond curls, five feet ten inches tall and loose-jointed, sitting easily as if comfortable with himself.

At my appearance, Mother and Dad say goodnight and retire upstairs. Seymour and I again fall into easy conversation, getting to know each other a little before he leaves as promised so that I can study my driver's manual. He's as attractive in person as he was on the phone.

I pass the driver's test just fine the next morning and earn my license. In the evening, while dancing during dinner, Seymour comments, "You're the first girl I've met who's enthusiastic about your job instead of whining." Born in the Bronx, New York, at twenty-seven years old he's happily living in the downtown Hartford YMCA and practicing optometry in the neighboring small town of Newington. He has the sweetest temperament I've ever encountered. I like the way he pronounces *perfect*, slightly drawing out the first syllable to sound like a contented cat, and that he fondly calls his middle-aged maroon Studebaker *the little kaputka*. Because he doesn't like swearing, he substitutes funny made-up exclamations like *Suzitsu!* I'm careful to temper the vocabulary I picked up in my theater years.

On our second date that week, as soon as he's helped me into the car and got behind the wheel, he hands me a package of Clorets with a charming apology: "I want to kiss you goodnight when I take you home later, but I don't like the smell of cigarette smoke." The girl my mother accuses of having a redheaded temper smiles serenely, removes a green tablet from the roll and pops it into her mouth. She smokes a little less during the evening and has no trouble at all exchanging a minty Cloret for a last cigarette at the end.

In the week after I get my driver's license, I drive to The Hartford every morning with Dad as my passenger, relinquish his car, and take the bus home after work. One time I drive Mother to the grocery without causing her any apparent trauma. This hardly makes me a seasoned veteran. Yet the next Saturday when Seymour collects me at the folks' and walks me to the *kaputka* parked at the curb, he opens the driver's door and with a sweeping flourish indicates a brand new cushion on the seat.

"I bought this for you," he crows, "So you can reach the steering wheel, because today you're going to drive us to the Bronx to visit my parents." With my brand new license, he's trusting me to navigate the interstate highways that now bypass New Haven and get us into New York in two hours! Without argument, I get behind the wheel. He does not backseat drive.

By the time we approach Grant's Tomb on New York's Riverside Drive, I become aware that our conversation has slowed to a standstill, and sneaking a glance to the right, I see that my companion has fallen asleep. The traffic at the tomb is not at a standstill. It's as thick and chaotic as I noted when a youngster, but I negotiate it with glowing confidence born of the trust my passenger's sleep demonstrates. By my own childhood definition, I have arrived as a pro—already!—thanks to him.

On Bryant Avenue in the Bronx, where Seymour's folks live, the brick apartment buildings crowd the sidewalks. There are no lawns and no garages. Cars are parked bumper to bumper along the curbs, and when a space is miraculously vacated, a tenant who's awaiting guests stands in the empty spot to hold it for them. Now awake, Seymour talks me into the space his father is thus reserving, and once out of the car, he introduces us.

Benjamin Fenster is an elderly retiree of medium height, still straight and handsome with a full head of well-behaved grey hair. I quickly see where his son's level temperament comes from. Mama, with her squat, spreading figure, is feisty but warm and welcoming, and both of them obviously adore their youngest child. Seymour's older brother and sister are not there today. The parents are unsophisticated Old World people but lovable. The visit goes well.

Our courtship breezes along until the wind abruptly goes out of my sails. We're in the audience at Bushnell Memorial Hall when the Hartford Symphony and its choir perform the American premiere of Carl Orff's sensuous Carmina Burana. The masterful performance of the rousing cantata excites—animates—THRILLS me to the point of babbling when it's over! Seymour remains on an even keel, as if he's just heard a Hayden symphony for the umpteenth time. This man is not a soul mate! The next day I tell Mother I'm losing interest in him; he's dull. But she has already fallen in love with him, and she counsels me to give him a chance because he has so many good qualities. For once I listen and gradually soften again.

In December, Gloria from my Boston ad agency

invites me to spend the weekend with her. She tells me that she and Ray, who've shared the agency's back office for years, are going to dinner Saturday night and why don't I have someone come up and double date? I'm surprised because the last I knew, Ray was engaged to another woman, but it's a great opportunity to do my Chanukah shopping in the Boston stores and reconnect with my friend. Seymour likes the idea of going out Saturday night in Boston and driving me home on Sunday.

I take the train up Saturday morning, and by the time I get to Gloria's apartment it's raining. She's out doing errands but has left me a key. Easily finding an umbrella, I start on my shopping rounds. As I walk toward Filene's, I'm attracted to a decorative ring in the window of a small jewelry store, and I stop in to ask the price from the proprietor. Although I can afford it, remembering that my mission is to buy presents for others, I thank him and leave without even trying it on. During the afternoon, I have good luck finding some perfect gifts for those on my list, but as I go from store to store, the rain gets increasingly harder and the umbrella becomes useless. Now soaked through, my route back to Gloria's leads me by the jeweler's again. Having completed my gift buying, I go back in to try on the ring. There are no other customers in the store. The instant the owner catches sight of me in the doorway, he launches into a scathing attack.

"You sure are self-centered! It's Christmas! When you should be thinking of buying for others, you're so selfish you only think of giving yourself a present!"

When I look down at the multiple paper shopping bags I'm carrying to shoot back, "What do you think these are?" I'm horrified to see that they're sopping and on the verge of disintegrating. I flee the shop and barely manage to reach Gloria's without the bags' totally collapsing and dumping their contents.

The painful truth is that I agree with the spiteful jeweler, and not only in reference to the holiday. No less than he, I have long castigated myself for being self-centered. Being thus brutally defined by another, I'm already sunk low when Gloria comes home. Now she confides that although Ray's still engaged to the woman wearing his ring, Gloria's own relationship with him is far from platonic. But her Catholic conscience is making her miserable, she whines. As far as I can tell, she's bouncing from Ray's bed every Saturday night to the confessional every Sunday morning and living in a constant state of guilt. I suggest that the decent thing to do is to move to a new job and quit being a partner in this two-timer's betrayal. How could I not have known that Gloria is no different from my old roommate Toni? I see that these are not my kind of people, I never really knew them, and I can't wait to go home.

When Ray shows up at the apartment, it's clear that he's already had a few guilt-suppressing drinks. I'm seriously out of my element here, and though I long for the cleansing presence of Seymour, I'm so sorry that he'll be involved in my error. In addition, the downpour outside has escalated, and I'm deeply concerned about his traveling two hours in driving rain. But by now he's already in his car, and there's no way to contact him. As much as I need him, I lay my head back on the sofa, close my eyes and silently pray, "God, don't let him come. Please let him be sensible enough to stay home." Repeating that prayer over and over inside my head, I slowly hear that for the first time in my life, I care more about someone else than I do for myself. I've never felt this way about anyone before, and a sense of wonder and gratitude overtakes me.

Exactly when he said he would, Seymour arrives. Amid my mixed feelings of joy and remorse, introductions are made and off we all go for dinner. As Ray has more to drink, he shrivels as a man. Seymour turns his chair toward me, plants his elbow on the table in front of me with his forearm raised, and resting his head on his open hand to block both our companions from my view and my mind, he engages my total attention with cheerful conversation. Magically, to the recorded background of My Funny Valentine, which becomes Our Song, he creates a place that we inhabit alone together. My prince has come. I realize that I love him and want to be with him for the rest of my life.

Ray leaves for his home and Seymour for the local Y right after taking us back to Gloria's. I go to sleep as ecstatic in my new knowledge as I was miserable before. Seymour picks me up in the morning, and on the ride home there is no need for a question to be asked and answered; we simply decide to have four children and not to keep a kosher home.

THE REVELATION

Soon after we first met, Seymour shared that in the past year he'd had a tumor biopsied at the Veterans Hospital, and it had been such a relief when the doctor assured him and his family that he did not have cancer! His initial symptoms disappeared with a course of radiation, giving him a clean bill of health. He was so grateful to be well and strong!

But as soon as I happily tell those close to me that we're going to be married, a call from a concerned friend of the family rips away my joy. Incredibly, this family friend discloses that although Seymour and his family were not told so, in truth he was diagnosed with Hodgkin's Disease and was not expected to live more than six months beyond the biopsy.

"But look how healthy he is! The radiation worked!"

"He's in remission. There is treatment, but there is no cure."

Where can I put such news? My mind scampers hither and thither but cannot find a place within me for the knowing.

If a caring person has uncovered a patient's private medical information and passed it along, is it then his responsibility to engineer the outcome of his revelation? I learn that the girl Seymour was dating before me was warned off by a VA nurse and quickly stopped seeing him. Now a new informer intends to have me follow. He is determined to protect me, my parents and my sister from heartbreak, but he is too late. Heartbreak already lies for me in the conspiracy swirling behind this cherished patient's back. Is my beautiful Seymour never to have love before he dies and never to know why?

It's got to be just a vicious rumor. Seymour has introduced me to warm friends who were there at the time of his surgery. When I seek them out alone at their home, they tell me that because they suspected the symptoms, they specifically asked his doctor if the diagnosis was Hodgkin's Disease and were emphatically assured that it was not. Further, Clara and Harvey reiterate, it was confirmed to Seymour and his parents that the biopsy had ruled out cancer. I have met his family and haven't sensed any hidden stress.

Nevertheless, Concerned Friend insists that he is correct and vows to alert my parents if I don't stop seeing Seymour. Not just a childish threat to tattle on me to mommy and daddy about some peccadillo, this is outright extortion that can ruin lives. Determined to find out the truth for myself, I join the rule-breaking brigade.

I know that the benign diagnosis was made by Dr. G. at the Veterans Hospital in New Haven, whom Clara has told me really came to love Seymour. I ask Harvey to go with me to the hospital. At the first floor information desk, when I inquire where I might find the doctor, I am too quickly told that he's unavailable. I stroll nonchalantly through the lobby and from the directory outside the elevator note his office number on the second floor. While Harvey distracts the guard with absorbing conversation, I slip up the stairs and find the good doctor in his office. He looks up surprised at his unannounced visitor.

"Doctor," I blurt out without preamble, "I'm in love with Seymour Fenster and want to marry him. I need to know if he has Hodgkin's Disease."

"Absolutely not!" Hippocrates' disciple explodes.

"Let me put it this way," I persist, "If I were your daughter, would you encourage me to marry him?"

"Absolutely!" he replies.

"AND HAVE CHILDREN?"

"Absolutely!"

There it is. I cannot believe that a man sworn to "First do no harm," no matter how much he loves his patient, would encourage a young woman to conceive a child destined to be fatherless at birth. With heart lifted, I go back downstairs, collect Harvey, and we happily drive home to reassure Clara that she's right and to convince my self-appointed protector that he's misinformed.

The next day my phone rings at work. "That doctor is a liar, and there are people in the medical community who are furious with him and have set him straight," says Concerned Friend. "He has lied to Seymour and lied to you, and if you don't stop seeing Seymour, we will have to tell *him* the truth."

I'm struck dumb with heart-splitting pain at the pronouncement and blazing outrage at the arrogant God-playing that is playing with my life. Who is this new "we"? How many are now threatening me? Battered and unable to function, I leave work, but there is nowhere to go to deal with my quandary but round and round inside my own head.

With this cauldron of deceit boiling furiously, how can its vapors fail to reach Seymour? The next day he calls me at The Hartford.

"Can you leave work now?" he asks. "I want to go to New Haven and talk to Dr. G., and I need you with me." I am stabbed with guilt; it's my entrance on the scene that has destroyed the innocent contentment this man knew before me.

He picks me up in the *kaputka* and asks me to drive. As we're on the Berlin Turnpike headed toward New Haven, it occurs to him that he'd better make sure the doctor is in today. I pull off into a dirt lot where he's spotted a pay phone, and he leaves the car to dial the hospital. We have no idea that he'll be put through directly to the man who has just been excoriated by his peers. But watching through the windshield, I see Seymour's whole body sag as he slowly hangs up and drags himself back to collapse into his seat. Oh, stupid, stupid, why was I not with him at the phone?

He reports: "Dr. G himself picked up the phone. I said Hello, this is Seymour Fenster, and he cut me off with 'If you want to know what you've got, it's Hodgkin's Disease, plain and simple!' and he slammed down the receiver."

That is the gentle manner in which my love is told that he is soon to die. We sit in that dirt lot and I hold him, but we have no place to go home to. He does not want to live out the rest of his life in the Bronx with his parents. I can no longer bear to stay with mine. Seymour and I must make a home together, however briefly.

THE DECISION

Of course I am not going to turn my back on this man. When that becomes clear, my parents are indeed informed of his condition. Though they ardently love him themselves, they instantly redouble the crushing pressure on me to leave him. I understand and ache for them as well as myself; I too would try to dissuade a daughter from a disrupted life. But I cannot do as they wish.

Seymour's sister Sarah understands his diagnosis. Their elderly parents, in the Old World tradition, know nothing of silent stoicism, and their flutterings of fear before the biopsy had intensified the burden of their American-born child. Therefore, after the exploration Seymour, his parents and his brother Harry were told only that he does not have "cancer," and only Sarah knows what comes after "but…"

I am tormented with questions. Before his diagnosis Seymour's twenty-seven years on earth seemed only a prelude to the rich and full life he anticipated. Was he to be told that he had only six months left of that life, to mourn all dreams, dread oncoming death but choose how he wanted to spend his remaining time? Was it better to hide the truth so that he could live happily unaware, free of fear, and full of hope? At the end might he not feel duped, lamenting what he might have done with the time had he known? Should one explain the truth to his aged parents and watch them live on the brink of tragedy or let them fully enjoy whatever time they have left of their son? Who was to make those decisions? I wasn't on the scene yet when the questions had to be answered, but I suspect Sarah made a merciful choice, only to have Judy and her family friend come along to unravel it. I am torn between guilt for that and gratitude for the chance to add love to Seymour's life before he must relinquish living. This is not a Saturday morning radio play, and I ask myself how long the secret could have been kept anyway before recurring pain and hospital stays revealed the horrible truth. Should Seymour then have been alone?

Now that he has learned his prognosis, I gently ask if there are any dreams he wishes to fulfill in the time left. I will support them. He answers, "There are only three things I've always wanted in life—to share love with a woman, to own my own home, and maybe have my own little office building." But now to protect me, he's afraid that my parents are right in opposing our marriage. We have not yet formally announced our engagement and I have no ring, but I will not even talk of our being apart before the ordained time has come.

The road will not be easy. Ever since my early teens when, visiting my mother after an operation, I heard the jarring moans from neighboring rooms and inhaled the nauseating smells, the very thought of a hospital has made me queasy. Will I be able to stiffen my spine and be good support to Seymour when he needs to go in for treatment? I am afraid. At the same time I sense that I'm being asked to do something by a power outside myself and will be given the strength I need. My piteous fears are immaterial.

I'm being mercilessly tugged apart by my family. My mother's emotional health is slipping, which is pulling Dad down, too. I hear her awake all night in their bedroom on the other side of my wall. By daylight she offers me a bribe: they will send me on an extended tour of Europe, which I know they can't afford, to provide me time and space to forget

Seymour. My father, understanding nothing from previous experience, bluntly orders me to stop seeing him. Another evening in the living room Mother dramatically drops to her knees before me and clasping her hands, tearfully begs me to give Seymour up. Looking at her there on the carpet, I'm torn between pity and the suspicion that it's a performance deliberately staged to manipulate me. I stifle the scream that wants to burst out of me, but I can't forestall the coming of my own wracking sobs. I am sorry for my shaken father to witness this melodrama. Helplessly, he calls Uncle Harold, who now lives around the corner with Aunt Rose. My dear uncle comes and takes me downtown to his chiropody office, where he has me immerse my bare feet in his soothing whirlpool tub and talks me down with his sane and sympathetic voice.

It is too awful to drag out any more. In spite of everyone's hopes, I understand that I will not belong to anyone else while I know that Seymour is on this earth. I propose to him that we mercifully end all the struggle by quickly getting married in New York. Then it will be done, and all the forces can quit scheming and making themselves physically and morally ill. And we will have the life together that is meant, however short.

Seymour sets one condition. I am young; I must promise that when the end comes I will not spend protracted time grieving but will go about building a new life and be open to another love. He knows that I keep my promises.

We tell Mama and Papa Fenster that since my parents don't want me to marry anyone yet, they will not make a wedding. But I think these folks are sharper and stronger than we've been giving them credit for. To secure their son's happiness, they ask no questions and contact their own rabbi, as we request. We set a date for a family wedding in the rabbi's Bronx apartment on the first Sunday after we get our marriage license. We do not notify my parents. I am heartsick for them that they will be absent, but I cannot risk

Mother's staging an excruciating last-ditch scene at the ceremony.

After quickly presenting ourselves to the New York lab for the required blood tests, Seymour and I begin counting the days till we can be made one. The next week while we're attending a friend's formal wedding at a Bronx catering hall, Seymour is called to the phone. His sister tells him that the lab has dropped our samples and we must give blood again. With time running down, we look in a phone book and find a private doctor around the corner from the caterer. We walk there at once, I in my silver brocade dress and high heels, Seymour in his dark suit, for once retaining its sharp crease. There are no other patients in the doctor's home office, and he welcomes us in right away. Without going into detail, we explain that our blood samples have been dropped just before our own wedding and that we are in a hurry to return to our friend's reception. The elderly doctor's eyes sweep over my flat stomach, but he still thinks he understands our desire for speed. He is softly paternal. As he draws my blood, he keeps soothing, "Everything will turn out all right. You'll see, everything is going to be all right, and you will have a good life." Though there is no way either of his assumptions could be true, I love that dear stranger for his caring.

On the Friday before our wedding, Seymour has rented a car and left for his folks' apartment, leaving me to drive the *little kaputka* to Harvey and Clara's. I am there to leave what I hope is a compassionate letter of explanation to be mailed to my parents on Saturday. March has come in like an angry lion, and everything is frozen. When I return to the *kaputka* parked in back of our friends' house, the windshield is covered with a layer of white ice too thick for the defroster to melt. Taking the scraper from the glove compartment, I think of the cruel thing I'm doing to my parents. I hurt from their pain and my pain. Standing in the snow, cut through by the freezing wind and chopping at the malevolent ice, I feel so alone. A girl should be in the warm embrace of joyful parents before her wedding. Instead I am alone and terribly cold. Cold and chopping and crying.

My groom and I are not to see each other the day before the wedding. Clara has arranged for me to stay with her and Harvey Saturday night at the Long Island home of her sister and brother-in-law, whom I've never met. There after a generously prepared celebratory dinner, the two sisters present me with a box wrapped in pretty wedding paper. Nestled in the tissue within are a wispy pink nightgown and negligee. This is as close to a bridal shower as I will come, and warm tears again fall at the kindness of Clara and a woman who has enough love to extend to her sister's friend.

Mama Fenster calls. She says, "I know you will not go to the *mikvah*, but I will be content knowing you'll take a hot shower." It must be hard for her to relinquish any demand for the Orthodox public ritual bath, but she is not going to make things any more difficult. God love her.

On Sunday morning when Seymour's immediate family, Clara, Harvey and the rabbi's wife gather with us in the rabbi's living room, we only count nine men present. The kindly *rebbe* goes out into the hall and asks a Jewish neighbor to come in to complete a *minyan*, the ten-man quorum necessary to perform a Jewish ritual. The ceremony, modified from the Orthodox, is not burdensome. Seymour and I become man and wife on March 6, 1955. He is twenty-seven years old; I am twenty-three. After the symbolic stomp breaking a napkin-wrapped glass tumbler by my groom and the calling of Mazeltov! by our guests, we are ushered into the rabbi's kitchen to be alone for the first time as newlyweds. We embrace and return to the living room, then are off with our guests to our wedding dinner at Gluckstern's kosher restaurant. My heart is full of gratitude for the loving arrangements my in-laws and Sarah have made.

Seymour is wiser than I. Alone in our hotel room

after the dinner, he expresses concern about my parents' being by themselves tomorrow when they read the letter telling of our marriage. He urges that we call Roan, break it to her gently, and ask her to relay the news in person. We never burdened my sister with our secret, but now yet another innocent is to be caught in our web. I understand Seymour's wisdom, and we make the call together. From the depths of her shock, Roan assures us that she will carry out the commission and wishes us well. Only then are we fully liberated to spend the night reveling in our newly married status.

It was right to end the struggle. Mollie and Dan Horowitz call upon the strength of character I've often witnessed and hoped would triumph this time. When we return to Hartford after our week's honeymoon in Manhattan, Mother opens their door to Seymour with outstretched arms. Gallantly, she affirms, "Now you are ours."

With heads held high, she and Dad soon host a champagne reception at the downtown Shangri La restaurant to introduce their son-in-law and his family to their friends and local relatives. The guests already think me impulsive and nonconformist, and since my petite size seven dress emphasizes my twenty-one-inch waist, it deflects any rude questions about the elopement. Mother regains her balance, Dad starts telling jokes again, and they both allow themselves to love Seymour as they had before they learned his awful secret. But my father brands me a liar and never again trusts me. He recedes even further from me, and the distance is never to be recovered.

EQUILIBRIUM

Seymour and I have come home to continue working and to take up residence in our attic apartment on Vine Street in Hartford. Unlike the Davis attic on Blue Hills Avenue, it has three discreet temperature-controlled rooms...but no secure entries. Inside the locked front door of the house, landings on the first and second floors lead to keyed doors into those flats, but at the top of the stairs we have no door. One walks through an open threshold straight into our living room with its convertible sofa, two easy chairs, end table, and storage closet. The back stairs end at the landing outside our kitchen where a pantry cabinet stands, but the door into the kitchen has no lock. Between kitchen and living room is our bedroom under the eaves, not luxurious but not cramped. Since the apartment comes furnished, we save money for a home of our own, however unrealistic, instead of outfitting a way station.

No one ever bothers us. If the good-natured landlady on the first floor wants to come up, she calls first. Since both Seymour and I work, we aren't home during the day, but none of our possessions are ever out of place when we return. Our downstairs neighbors are busy with their own lives in the evenings, and we feel no threat to privacy in our little aerie.

The eat-in kitchen is ample and well-equipped, allowing us to have friends in for dinner. Seymour is apt to issue impromptu invitations at the eleventh hour. It doesn't give me much time to plan or prepare, but I cater to his gregarious spontaneity as to everything that is a part of him. I'm proud to meet the challenge; I want him to eke out every drop of enjoyment from whatever time he has on earth.

When I contemplate life without him, though I desperately try to keep such thoughts at bay, it is so unthinkable that I come to consider our gas stove as a potential tool to help me go with him when the time comes. But I am only twenty-three years old, and am I not the one who rails against disdaining God's gifts? I remind myself that the greatest of these is life. I also remind myself that I've made Seymour a promise, and so I determine to stay rooted in the present, where we have each other.

You'd never mistake my husband for a city slicker. In spite of the tailor's every effort, his trousers refuse to hold a crease, and his favorite brown tweeds droop formlessly on his legs, slumping as if too long at his shoe tops. The Bronx-born boy looks every inch the country doctor, a son of Newington.

When he first arrived, his gentle friendliness made him a favorite of all the small town shopkeepers and professionals along Main Street and Market Square. Once his awful prognosis leaked out of the local Veterans' Hospital on the hill, where care was transferred after surgery and radiation, these good townspeople imbedded him in their hearts as their own. Though they now discreetly keep their own counsel, I sense the shock when we announce our marriage. A few visibly disapprove of his sharing his fate with an innocent, some wonder if my motives *are* innocent, but I feel that most bless me for standing with him.

I don't get into Newington too often, because we only have the one car. I ride the bus to and from work in Hartford and start preparing dinner as soon as I get home. But when I do walk along the sidewalk connecting the storefronts in Newington, what a warm feeling when tenants come to their doors to greet me with a very personal, "Hello, there, Mrs. Fenster." I quickly change that to "Judy," and I just as quickly fall in love with these folks. The long block of Main Street between Cedar Street and Market Square is presided over on one side by the brick Congregational church with its lofty steeple. Across the street is Seymour's optometric office, the barber, a hardware store, and a few other offices and shops. By town decree, the architecture of every building around the corner on Market Square is Colonial, unifying and preserving the flavor of the community. On the south side are the town newspaper office, the pharmacy, the venerable family doctor who makes house calls, and the modern pediatrician who doesn't. The north side is dominated by the bright, spacious Nutmegger restaurant, where families feel comfortable enjoying superior fare and where Rotary and Kiwanis hold their monthly meetings.

Seymour belongs to Kiwanis, and I'm fond of the other wives. But it isn't until I rearrange one gal's hair at a party and reminisce about getting down in the mud to dig clams that I feel their acceptance of me as a real person. At last just One of Us! Horns exclaim! Drums resound! Dancers leap and angels sing! I've won my Olympic tug of war with my lady mother!

Boston and New York are exciting and Hartford is boring, once rightly described by *Look* magazine as "tight, tidy, tolerant and tiresome." But with a population of twelve thousand split between descendants of Yankee farmers and an influx of up-and-comers whose homes now occupy the expansive old farmland, Newington snuggles itself into a special corner of my heart, where it remains forever.

Seduced by such a kind and peaceful aura, it is possible for stretches of time to ignore the sword of Damocles dangling above us. Seymour is blessed with an extended remission, and when the six-month mark approaches without dire forebodings, we allow ourselves to believe that a miracle is in progress.

RELAPSE

We're grateful for an ordinary day-to-day routine that makes us feel just like people who have an unclouded life. Except there are a few differences. I go to sleep every night with my hand resting lightly on Seymour's groin; it's the last loving touch before sleep, yes, but it also allows me to secretly reassure myself that the lump in that lymph node is not growing.

I also make sure that not too much time goes by between visits with his family. Because it's difficult for them to travel to Hartford, in winter we see them in the Bronx and in summer at their cottage on Lake Waubeka in Danbury, Connecticut. The first time we get into swimwear to sit by the lake, Seymour pulls on a tee shirt. A long, angry scar from his biopsy curves from just under his rib cage around onto his back. In addition, radiation treatments to his lungs have burned a permanent red box the size of a single electrical socket below the base of his neck. He hasn't been on a beach since those procedures, and he now considers, "People sure won't want to look at my scars."

I counter, "You have a right to feel the sun on your body. If anyone has trouble with your chest, that is truly their problem and not yours. They can just look away." He swaps the tee shirt for sunscreen, and we spend an uneventful afternoon swimming in the lake and basking on our beach blanket. No one stares at his bare chest; no one comments;

no one goes shrieking off the beach. I'm so glad that I'm here, so grateful that I'm able to liberate my husband from unwarranted shame.

Seymour can make any little outing an adventure. Just going around the corner with him is fun. We take little drives, browse quaint shops, visit charming local sites, performances, exhibits and fairs—just generally enjoying life. In the summer of 1955 we venture further afield to vacation at Niagara Falls. We view the spectacular American and Canadian cascades from overlooks on both sides, don the raincoats provided to walk behind them on a wet ledge, and get thoroughly sprayed as we approach them head-on aboard the little Maid of the Mist boat. We have a memorable lunch on the balcony of The Refectory in Queen Victoria Park, across the road midway between the two falls. The spray from the roaring water carries all the way across the street and drops gently upon us as we savor well-prepared food. It makes us laugh.

We continue on toward Toronto, Canada, and the next day swim in Lake Erie right outside our motel. We enjoy the British flavor of Toronto, buy some lovely bone china, and take afternoon tea in a large department store downtown. In the evening we see The Glenn Miller Story at a theater near our motel. Before the film starts we immerse ourselves in the spirit of the British Empire by respectfully rising with the rest of the audience to sing God Save the Queen. It's fun to feel almost as if we have crossed the Atlantic.

Seymour decides to cover the entire three-hundred-sixty-five miles back home the next day. Though I'm prepared to share the driving, he refuses any help. He insists that he enjoys being behind the wheel and isn't getting tired. With the windows open all the way, a nice breeze keeps us comfortably cool. Stopping only for lunch, we're home before dark and happy to tumble into bed early.

In the morning Seymour awakens with an aching neck. I kick myself for letting him drive too long with the breeze blowing directly on him. We are cruelly punished for this error in judgment when it becomes apparent that this is more than a simple stiff neck. He has pushed his immune system too far, and there is to be no more miracle; Hodgkin's Disease has reappeared.

The next treatment for Hodgkin's is a course of nitrogen mustard. Since its side effect is violent and prolonged vomiting, the patient must be hospitalized. Seymour finally lets me drive, this time to the Newington Veterans Hospital. The question I agonized over before we married is quickly answered: I am so focused on my husband that if there are disturbing sights or sounds from other patients, they don't get through to me. There is no question that I will sit beside Seymour's bed until the medication takes effect and then repeatedly dash with him into the next room, where a deep, wide sink is waiting for his overwhelming nausea to come to its wracking climax. While he is being sick, I place my hand on his forehead to hold his head up, as my mother held mine when I was a child. Each time it happens so fast that a nurse reaches his side only when he's back in bed and I have washed his face with a wet cloth.

The treatment is administered in piecemeal doses over a five-day period. Each day I stay with Seymour until visiting hours are over, and at night I return to our Vine Street attic. My parents urge me to sleep at their house, but I want to be where my husband and I live together. When at first I feel uneasy, I remind myself of the year living in my Beacon Street walk-up—I'm an old hand at sleeping alone behind unlocked doors. *Besides*, I ask myself, *who knows you are up here? Anyone bent on evil would have to specifically be looking for a lone woman in an unlocked attic.* I manage to sleep and be ready to return to the hospital the next morning.

Nitrogen mustard may be vicious, but it effects another remission, and after the five-day course of treatment, Seymour and I both return to work and a life imitating normalcy. We are able to shut the memory of the ordeal behind a firmly closed door except for the infrequent nights when he wakes in pain. Then I sit up, turn on the light, and begin to talk with him about the wonderful places we've been and things we've done while I silently pray, "Please make the pain stop, please make the pain stop" until, mercifully distracted, he falls back to sleep.

THE APPLE TREE

Martin Luther said, "Even if I knew the world would perish tomorrow, I'd still plant an apple tree today." In that spirit, Seymour and I use a VA mortgage to buy a little Cape Cod style house in Elmwood, the modest enclave of West Hartford tucked away on the border of Newington. Our home has two bedrooms, a living room with fireplace, separate dining room, and kitchen. A short breezeway connects the jalousied back porch to the one-car garage. The attic behind the dormers is unfinished, but the basement has ample room to house a workshop for Seymour. Turning one bedroom into a TV den, the house is perfect for us. We're pleased with the new-looking wallpapers and carpeting that are already there. It's fun finding furnishings to fit, and Seymour enjoys building some cabinets and bookcases to fill nooks and corners. Our pleasure mounts when Harvey and Clara buy an almost twin house nearby, occasioning frequent visits back and forth.

Our Federal Street neighbors are enjoyable people, natural and friendly. I'm surprised to find living next door my Phi Sigma Sigma "mother" Sandy, who mentored me through pledging six years ago. I haven't seen her since I left UConn. On our other side lives Doris, who drives to work near The Hartford every morning and drops me off on her way. I get out earlier than she does and take the bus home. Seymour and I like both women and their husbands and take pleasure in getting to know all the other folks up and down our short block.

We are privileged to take three more vacations. We share the driving to Woods Hole on Cape Cod, where we catch the ferry to Martha's Vineyard. There we breathe deeply of the salt air as we wander among the fishing boats and walk the island from one end to the other, photographing each other against the nautical background. How peaceful!

Another time we rent a cabin at a camp on Lake George, New York, and do some fishing ourselves. With newly-met friends we take a motorboat out on the lake and enjoy the scenery. When I catch a fish, veteran campers show Seymour how to scale and bone it. Bare-chested, he chops wood for our fire ring. As he raises the ax, my heart swells to see his body looking so vibrant and strong!

But months later another relapse shatters our peace. We feel we must now alert his parents that he's ill. Their daughter Sarah brings them to visit him in the hospital, but before they can witness a nausea attack, I lead them all home to Federal Street for dinner. I've never had anyone follow me even in daylight, and, shaky with my own unhappiness, I constantly check my rearview mirror to be sure I haven't lost them in the dark. How can I know what's behind me any better than what's ahead of me?

We still do not voice their son's terminal prognosis to the Fensters, and right after dinner, Sarah whisks them back to the Bronx. My mother again suggests that I sleep at her house, but now behind locked doors in my own home, I'm even less nervous than on Vine Street. In five days Seymour returns and we again pick up our life.

When Mother can't help confiding his condition to Uncle Abe and Aunt Blanche in December 1956, they invite Seymour and me to be their guests for a week at the Betsy Ross Hotel in Miami Beach. Wishing to be hands-on managers, they've made their own home in a kitchenette unit at the hotel.

Uncle Lou, infirm from years of ignoring diabetes, can no longer manage the Ritz Carlton, and he and Aunt Dora have moved into the Betsy Ross. I'm told that Dora has evolved from a small-town matron to a rotund, white-haired denizen of the leisure life who now spends her days smoking cigars, going to the horse races, and playing pinochle with a circle of Good Ol' Boys. We don't see much of her, but we're delighted on arrival to find Uncle Lou sitting in the lobby, still looking dapper, still softly singing "dye-dee-dye" behind his neat mustache, as he did in my childhood. He calls us his darlings and immediately hands Seymour the keys to his car, saying "It's yours for the week. Go exploring." But first Uncle Abe and Aunt Blanche's son Larry gives us a tour in his own car of the glitzy ocean-side community. It sure is different from the sleepy town where my cousin June and I rang the doorbell of two dancing sisters all those years ago! After learning to speak fluent Spanish, Larry's an official guide for the influx of Cuban visitors, and he leaves nothing out of our tour. We feel enveloped by the warmth of my extended family's generous love. Yet once they have oriented us, they give us the great gift of privacy. They have no expectations and tell us we're free to be on our own as much as we wish.

My aunt and uncle have assigned us a big, beautiful room overlooking the ocean, sand, and palm trees across the street. Refugees from the New England winter, Seymour and I gratefully spend hours every day soaking up the sun on the beach. In addition to swimming in the Atlantic, we spend a couple of mornings in the hotel's patio pool, where the family does check up on us. We take leisurely walks around the neighborhood and follow recommendations to some great restaurants, quickly learning to carry sweaters against the zealous air-conditioning in every indoor space. We do not overlook the synagogue and delicatessen.

No trip to Miami Beach would be complete without picking oranges right off the trees and watching native

Floridians wrestle alligators. My uncles direct us to the jai alai fronton. Our eyes pop as the small, hard, round *pelota* no sooner whizzes into the wicker *cesta* strapped onto a player's arm than it's flung out again at almost two hundred miles per hour to ricochet off the surrounding walls. Holy cow!

One day as we enter the elevator outside our fourth floor hotel room, it's already crowded. We stand face to face just behind the door. As the cage descends, a man next to us loudly, crudely, and cruelly berates his wife. His voice becomes harsher and more threatening at each floor, but all the other occupants are shocked into silence. I sense rather than see my husband, maintaining a pleasant smile, imperceptibly drift away from me. I don't know how he does it, but when the door opens on the first floor, the loud bully is surprised to find an innocent Seymour's five-foot-ten-inch frame standing solidly in front of him long enough to politely let his wife and all the other ladies off the elevator first. The beleaguered woman rapidly disappears across the lobby and out the door before her puzzled husband can emerge. That is so Seymour. I remember his putting himself between me and our offending companions in that Boston restaurant the night I knew I was in love. Oh, God, if only I could find a way to block what is threatening him!

Like life, Florida weather is predictable in its unpredictability. A world of sunshine will suddenly be invaded by a powerful downpour, which within half a day will just as suddenly retreat to leave an uncontested field to the sun again. We experience only one of such days, but in spite of hoisting umbrellas and stubbornly carrying on, our special-needs spirits can't help sagging a bit under the weight of the gloomy sky. The next day that sky is wrung out, and we bounce back...until in early afternoon Seymour begins coughing and experiencing a sore throat. Since that is the way relapses have begun, terror sets in. We find the address of the Miami Veterans Hospital in the phone book and drive there. Mercifully, we don't have to wait too long before the examining doctor reports that Hodgkin's Disease is not responsible for Seymour's discomfort; he has simply caught a cold. We should be jubilant, but we're so worn out from fear that our gratitude is just quiet and fathomless.

Aunt Blanche has invited us to dinner in their quarters the same night. Fortunately neither she nor Uncle Abe ask us how we've spent the day. Blanche folds out a small table in the sitting room and serves the four of us a lavish soup-to-nuts dinner prepared in her little kitchenette. She's a petite, pretty woman with a fair complexion, well-coiffed yellow-gold hair, and elegant tastes. Years ago she and my uncle gave up a roomy home and intriguing garden in New Haven, Connecticut, to move here, and I marvel at what a good sport she is to make this diminutive space her castle without complaint. My admiration triples when she washes our dinner dishes in the small bathroom sink and sets them in a drain tray atop a towel on the closed toilet lid for me to pick up and dry. Sharing her whimsical outlook, it's really kind of fun.

At the end of the week, tan and rested except for our brief scare, we board the plane home. I'm thinking how lucky we are to be a part of my mother's warm and generous Libman family and to have our own comfortable home to come back to.

THE THIRD DREAM

At age twenty-eight, Seymour has now fulfilled two thirds of his stated life's dreams—the love of and for a woman and our own home to live in. We return from Florida to find fortune beaming upon the third vision—owning a little office building.

The town's elderly tailor, Sy Kaplan, and Seymour are warm friends who have shared their memories and dreams since Seymour's arrival in Newington. Sy owns the free-standing, one-story Colonial brick building at the head of Market Square, which houses his tailor shop. As soon as we return from Miami Beach, he calls to say that he is headed *to* Florida. He plans to close up shop and spend the rest of his days relaxing in retirement heaven, and he wants to give us the first chance to buy his building. He has ample savings and wants just enough money from the property to help him live moderately in Florida. He offers to carry a long-term mortgage himself with easy monthly payments.

Seymour talks to me about it, and Lord, it's financially frightening! We already have a home mortgage. If I really lose my husband, can I do it by myself? I've never thought about owning property other than a home. Let's see, I'd have to sell the optometry practice and would have those proceeds along with Seymour's Army insurance. The office would only take up half of Sy's building, and if I could rent out the other half, there'd be that income.

Then all of a sudden I leave off computing and become calm. My heart says, *This is one of only three things this man has ever wanted in his life. I came into our marriage with nothing, and if I lose the building, I'll be no worse off than when we started.* We sign the papers and move Seymour's practice into our own building. I buy café curtains for the many-paned front windows, and we engage a real estate agent to rent out the unused space.

We have planted another apple tree.

THE END OF THE MIRACLE

Remissions are becoming shorter and relapses more frequent and virulent. Once again I'm on my way out of Seymour's hospital room when his Newington doctor catches up with me.

"I need to talk with you," he says. "His time is getting shorter."

"Yes, I know."

"If you want to have a baby, you don't have much time to get pregnant."

I know he is trying to be helpful and kind. Inside my head I say, *Dear doctor, we have been married for almost two years. Do you think we have not discussed this?* Aloud I say, "Thank you, doctor."

Again Seymour fights back and is released. We pray that our love is strong enough to keep holding him here, but we are losing the battle. The malevolence which has been kept from returning to his lungs now breaches the barrier. The next time I'm allowed into his hospital room, I find him surrounded by an oxygen tent. I cannot hold his hand; I sit near the foot of the bed and hold his toe. He isn't breathing easily enough to say much, and though I've been able to talk him through pain and fear before, in the presence of the intimidating plastic tent, tank, and hose, I have to dig deep to come up with an encouraging smile and diverting conversation. He talks to me in sign language, pointing up to

God, to me, to his heart, and to his wedding band. I tell him that I love him, that God loves him, and that I thank God for giving us to each other. He smiles but tires quickly, and I must leave him to sleep.

Our loyal friend Harvey has insisted that I meet him for a respite lunch. I leave the hospital, only to find that apprehension and guilt make a sour sauce for food. On my way out, the doctor walks me to my car and asks if he may have a minute with me. As I get behind the wheel, he sits in the passenger seat and turns to me. His voice, more teacher than comforter, pins me in that enclosed space.

"I'm sorry," he says. "He hasn't much longer."

"Yes." *Why am I always hearing devastating news in a car?*

"If you want a child, there's no time to waste." *That again.*

"We have made our decision."

Long ago we agreed not to decide for a powerless child that he or she be born without the father other children take for granted. There will be no child to wonder why he or she is the only one to attend father/child events with a surrogate daddy. In spite of my promise, there can be no guarantee that there will be an inspiring male role model at home.

Seymour will not have me go through a pregnancy and delivery alone. He will not have me raise a child alone. He has made me promise I'll be open to another love, and he cannot bear to think of a child of his giving pause to a man who might want to marry me or that I might be tempted to marry for the child's security.

With pity for the unborn and love for each other, we have agreed to leave this one apple tree unplanted.

One more time the miracle intervenes. Seymour rallies, and I'm able to take him home to act out a life again. But too quickly the night comes when he starts coughing more harshly than before, and when I take the Kleenex from him, I see the dreaded signal I have been warned about. The miracle cannot save us now; he is coughing up blood. As I've been instructed, I call 911, and the ambulance comes to take us to the hospital. At 2:00 the next morning the last of this beautiful man's life slips away.

DENIAL

I am sitting in the family room at Weinstein's Mortuary that is shielded from the larger congregation of mourners. I can view Rabbi Silverman conducting the funeral from the altar, while Seymour lies in the coffin selected by Dad and Howard on the level below. He is clothed in the brown tweed suit I loved best on him. The trousers are not bagging now on his still form.

How did this service come to be? I know that in a dazed state I was asked questions, I made choices, and my father and brother-in-law completed the arrangements with the suave Weinstein brothers. My mind only awakened when Rabbi Silverman came to me in this room to pin a black faille-covered button on my dress, reciting a prayer as his razor cut a symbolic slash in the button's short attached ribbon. Before that did Howard make that difficult call to Seymour's sister in New York? Did I call Clara to start the telephone tree so that friends and relatives could attend the funeral within twenty-four hours according to Orthodox law? How did I get to the mortuary?

Now as I direct my attention away from these questions toward the rabbi on the pulpit, I feel the firm pressure of Seymour's hand on my shoulder. I hear him whisper "Hi, Zeesa." The word, in Galician-accented Yiddish, means "sweet one" and is his pet name for me. I so strongly feel him standing just behind me that I don't have to

248 / Judy Horowitz Fenster Lovins

look back. I'm grateful to be hidden from those good friends who are fighting tears in the main chapel as I softly smile at the secret I share with my husband. Who would understand a young widow smiling at her husband's funeral? But he has come to me, and I now know that he will be with me as long as I need him.

Under the awning at the cemetery, I sit silently in the front row of chairs next to the grave. Someone else has made these arrangements, and I don't immediately see where my in-laws are. But as the burial service starts, Mama Fenster cries out pitifully. She continues shouting her grief while the rabbi impassively intones prayers amid the obscene creaking of the rollers lowering her son forever away from her caress. My sophisticated New World rabbi raises his head uncomfortably from his prayer book and tries to silence her unsettling outcries with a forbidding look. I throw him a forbidding frown of my own. I want to yell at him, "That is her culture's way of expressing unbearable grief, and who are you to reproach her?" I wish I were sitting beside Mama to put my arms around her. It may be that when my heart allows me to admit the truth, I will be screaming myself.

Because Seymour died in the Veterans' Hospital, his casket has been draped with an American flag. Who did this without consulting or warning me? Just before the coffin is lowered, two men in uniform remove the flag with precise tradition, folding it corner to corner into a neat, tight triangle. One of them places it in my lap, looks me fully in the face, and pronounces, "From a grateful nation." I am so taken aback, I want to hit him. Seymour was drafted into a peacetime Army and served his time in the States. The Army issued him life insurance, and when he got sick, the Veterans Administration provided unlimited care. Later the V.A. helped our dream come true with their benevolent home mortgage. Our nation has been so good to us, it is I who should be expressing gratitude. Yet I do not even know who these strangers are who have taken it upon themselves to intrude their tradition into my own without my permission.

By the time all the well-wishers have drifted away, it's late in the day. The Fenster family has a two-hour ride back to the Bronx for a week of Orthodox observance in their own home. We embrace as they start their journey, and I am delivered to my parents' home for a week of less stringent ritual. Each of us has loved Seymour in our own way, and each of us must now find our own way to accept the unacceptable truth.

SHIVAH

Because my home can't accommodate as many visitors and because I envision emotional support from my parents, I agree to observe Memorial Week at their house. To be available to consoling family and friends from morning through evening, it is easier to sleep there for the week. Mistake! After being mistress of my own home for two years, I am less equipped than ever to live under the same roof with my mother and father.

The tradition of *sitting shivah* is wise, keeping the bereaved surrounded by company until the first shock of the loved one's death wears off and the real business of coping begins. At night after everyone has left, there is nothing to protect me from the unbearable truth. But I am so depleted by the day's socializing that almost as soon as the grief threatens to wash back over me, I dissolve into sleep.

I don't cry; I deny. How cold-hearted well-wishers must think me, acknowledging their sympathy with a smile, chatting and even laughing with them. The only feeling that gets through is the abrasion of Mother's playing the perfect party hostess. My friends and hers bring gifts of sweets, for which I thank them before setting them aside. On her own, Mother opens the candy boxes, arranges the pieces tastefully in her prettiest company dishes and graciously offers them around. What is this, a birthday? Then I realize that it is a feminine instinct to entertain in her own home, and I fault myself for not being in mine.

Though my mind must always rush heartbreak into a mental anteroom to be dealt with later, it is not so easy for my folks. Frankly, they came to love and approve of Seymour more than they do me, and no forewarning could shield them from the pain of losing a son. I regret my failure to appear suitably distraught when Mother accuses me across the breakfast table, "You have ice water in your veins." Several times during the week when no one's around and some little thing I do or don't do displeases her, she flings at me, "THAT'S WHAT SEYMOUR DIDN'T LIKE ABOUT YOU." Her arrow misses its mark, for I know that Seymour loved me, but I am astonished at the spectacle of a mother aiming for the jugular of her own child.

So where is Dad? I hear Mother squabbling with him from time to time and it hurts, remembering that Seymour and I argued only once from the time we met. When you've been given limited time, you fill it with love and leave no space for anger. I recall that after a project upstairs, Seymour often left his workshop tools on a small kitchen counter he'd made. It was right under a hanging quartet of shiny copper-bottomed pots. I explained that I took pride in burnishing those pots to a sparkle after each use, and I requested that he not spoil the display with grimy tools. When he kept forgetting, I was loth to nag. One day before he came home from his office, I took my gleaming pots down to the basement and scattered them on his worktable. Later when he went downstairs, I heard his sweet laughter. We spoke not one word about it, but I never found his tools in the kitchen again. And I got him to stop draping the day's discarded shirt on the nearest doorknob by hanging a pair of my panties on every door in the house. I remember only laughter and lovemaking, not skirmishing words. Of course, my parents are living a normal life free from the threat of imminent loss. Their bickering this week may be caused by the stress I've visited upon them, but it is the one thing that threatens to overwhelm my defense system and evoke tears I'm not ready for.

What I would like this week are my father's arms around me, his once loving voice soothing my anguish with a little gentle humor. But having visited his own grief upon him, I guess I don't deserve that.

On a brisk afternoon during the week, a taxi pulls up in my folks' half-frozen driveway. An older woman emerges on crutches, skirting random ice patches to reach our door while the cab pulls away. A widow, she lives alone a few houses down across the street and is returning from a doctor's appointment. I've never met Mrs. Kaplan, nor are my parents socially friendly with her. It would have been so much wiser in this unseasonable weather to have the driver take her directly home, and I am infinitely touched by her effort to reach out to us. She brings something more valuable than candy—the encouragement she offers me from her own experience is uplifting. When she collects her coat to leave, I reach into the closet for mine. Mother comes running.

"Where are you going?" she demands.

"To take Mrs. Kaplan home; the driveways are slippery. I'll be right back."

Mother's voice shakes. "You can't go out during Shivah!"

Oh! There it is again—commandment trumping compassion.

"Do you think God wants me to risk this kind woman's not reaching home safely so that I can adhere to some man-made rule? Shame on me if I do!"

"But you don't go out of the house during Shivah!"

"I do."

Of course an embarrassed Mrs. Kaplan is bound to say there's no problem, she'll be fine. Luckily, another guest becomes aware of the muted scuffle and with no further to-do drives her the two houses down, escorting her safely to her door. Seymour would have been the first to do that.

I can't look at Mother. I begin watching the flame on the *Yahrzeit* candle that burns for exactly a week in its glass jar, and I can't wait to be out of there.

Soothing comes from a surprising source. As the time draws to a close, Mama Fenster phones from the Bronx to tell me of a tradition she rightly guesses I don't know— *neshumah b'glayten*. When I remind her of my limited Yiddish, she urges in English, "When the candle flame burns out, leave the house and take your soul for a walk." I do. Alone. And then I go home—*my* home—to cry.

DENIAL DENIED

I'm so glad to be home, I could kiss the walls! I unpack, do laundry, and pick up the home and office mail that's been held at the post office. Each communication starting "Dear Dr. Fenster" cruelly drives home that my dear Dr. Fenster is no longer with me. So many reminders, so many decisions, so many connections to notify. And I must quickly acknowledge the kindness of all those caring people, known in many different ways—some even unknown—who have sent a flood of touching condolences. After a long day I put fresh linens on the bed and lie down to sleep on Seymour's half. It would be unbearable to wake on my side and see his place empty.

When I return to work the next day, my colleagues at The Hartford welcome me back with understanding yet wisely don't tip my balance with an oppressive weight of sympathy. Immersing myself in the work I love is a blessing. But walking from my desk to the water fountain after lunch, I become aware that my lips are moving soundlessly. I stop to pay attention to my silent mouthings and catch myself trying to determine what office to visit and what forms to complete to convince the Veterans' Administration that they've made a mistake and must give my husband back.

At night I dream that I prevail and am notified that he will be sent home. Standing by a roadside, I watch a small plane land in a field. Seymour emerges and starts down the road toward me with his warm smile. Imagine my wild elation! But as I watch him approach, a car races down the road and slams into him, killing him before my eyes. Now that I actually see him die again, I *must* believe it, mustn't I? Still I stubbornly don't cry. A few nights later I have the same dream. And another night. And yet again. How many dreams must I witness before I convince myself that he's not coming back?

Tradition forbids me to visit Seymour's grave for the first month, but then I have good occasion to do so. Upon my return to work, I join the Girls Club golfers. I play with a set of clubs that Seymour infrequently used, which are, of course, too big for me. I've never taken a lesson; my only practice is a rare visit to a driving range. Needless to say, I pockmark the city golf course with divots, taking heart in great progress only when I break one hundred...for nine holes. Because the course is directly across the street from the Emanuel Synagogue Cemetery, I can drive over after every weekly outing to talk with Seymour. I sit on the ground next to the rectangle where he lies, idly pulling a few weeds from the grass while we commune.

When I learn that the adjoining plot has been purchased, I come apart. In spite of my promise to go on with my life, it is I, not a stranger, who must be buried beside my husband! The synagogue's cemetery committee must void any contrary transaction! But for once my father comes to my rescue. He and Howard arranged together for Seymour's single plot, and Dad gently convinces me that Seymour wanted me to be buried beside a new, lifelong husband. Invoking my promise to build a new life, he slowly defuses me.

As spring progresses, I get out my trowel to work on my Federal Street plantings. Walking out my front door, I'm arrested by the jubilant green of the awakened grass and the show-off pink of the flowering almond bush at the corner of the driveway. My heart soars! Then it plummets. What kind of woman am I to take pleasure in these things when Seymour can no longer enjoy them?

Harvey and Clara are supportive beyond reason, and I abuse their generosity unforgivably. I buy a large Paint-by-Numbers canvas and keep it at their house with the brushes and paints. Every evening for a couple of months I drive there after dinner and spend the evening with them, painting while we chat or watch TV. But occasionally I get in the *kaputka* and drive aimlessly for hours on dark roads—anywhere, nowhere—till I'm calmed and ready for sleep. Other times we three go on a short day trip or eat out, and my friends are always respectful enough to let me attend to my own bill. They upheld me before Seymour and I were married, and they are upholding me now. When that support becomes no longer necessary, I do not know how to express the enormity of my gratitude, and I fall way short. I am afraid they will never know how much they have meant to me.

Seymour silently told me at the funeral that he would be with me as long as I need him, and he's as good as his word. With the weather warming up, I treat myself to a respite. Clad in shorts and a summer top, I lie on a beach towel in my back yard next to the breezeway, close my eyes, and welcome the sun on my body. I am totally concentrated on its soothing touch when I feel Seymour lying beside me on another towel. He says nothing. We don't need to talk, but I know he is there and as long as I don't open my eyes, he will remain. I think he's telling me it is time to go on without him. Oh, no, darling, please don't ask it of me yet. It is so soon.

The next Saturday while I'm shopping in the Finast grocery, I'm surprised to see a carton of sour cream in my hand. I am just about to put this favorite of Seymour's in my cart, anticipating his enjoyment. I stop short and stare at the carton. At last I tell myself *I don't like sour cream, and he is not here.* I put the carton back on the shelf.

Now hearing his voice in my head, sensing his presence is not enough. I ache to touch him! I ache to feel his arms around me, to sleep next to him and to awake with him! I want us to laugh together again, to plan together, and oh, I want to hear him say *purr-fect* like a contented kitten. I spend all Sunday afternoon curled on the den sofa sobbing to God, "I want him back! I want him back! I want him back!" I have finished my cowering and allowed the pain. The tears have come.

Starting Over

RICHARD

In June, 1955 after completing Army service as an optometrist for two years, Richard Lovins, O.D., twenty-seven years old, set up private practice in Westport, Connecticut. Raised in Bridgeport, Richard knew that Westport was an upscale town, but he wished he'd realized that with its proximity to New York, most of the affluent populace would only patronize the fashionable doctors and boutique eye salons in the Big Apple.

Though unhappy with the slow growth of his upstairs practice, professional and personal ethics kept him from advertising himself like the long ensconced practitioner whose commercial display of eyeglasses filled a storefront window not far off. After almost two years, if Richard wanted to support himself, he needed to act. He considered looking in other parts of the state to relocate or to buy a going practice. But because human nature delays the final acknowledgment of our mistakes, he was only toying with the idea.

After months of such dilly-dallying, early on the morning of April 4, 1957, Richard awoke with a new determination. "Today," he resolved, "I *will* look for a new location." Right after breakfast he drove sixty miles to the town of New Britain. Although he'd never been there, it sounded quaint and Colonial, like New England. What he found was the unromantic industrial city where Stanley tools are manufactured. But as long as he was there, he paid a visit to the local eye doctor to ask about the general area and any practice that might be for sale.

Dr. Macy picked up the morning newspaper and showed Richard the obituary of the twenty-nine-year-old optometrist in the neighboring town of Newington who had passed away during the night. He surmised that his successful practice would come on the market soon. With the office address in hand, Richard drove over to see the place, and what a pleasant surprise! Newington was the charming Colonial town he'd been envisioning, with the tall white steeple of the Congregational church presiding over Main Street. Richard reached the address he'd been given, looked in the window, and was confused to find the space devoid of equipment and personnel. He got back in his car and headed out of town. This was just his first stab at a mission he wasn't so sure about, anyway. He'd think about it some more and maybe venture out elsewhere another day.

But as he drove toward the town line Richard began to remonstrate with himself. "Idiot!" he exclaimed aloud. "Why didn't you go in and ask the barber next door what happened to the office?" He made a U-turn and hurried back. Once again parking his car on Main Street, he entered the barbershop to ask if anyone knew where Dr. Seymour Fenster's practice was. "Oh," said the barber, "He bought his own building and moved onto Market Square a couple of months ago." And so Richard rounded the corner and found Dr. Fenster's sign in front of a free-standing one-story Colonial cottage. He was charmed by the blue-checkered café curtains hanging in its front windows under a sheltering maroon-and-white-striped metal awning.

When Dr. Fenster had suddenly gone into the hospital, a retired optometrist who'd covered for him during prior confinements had stepped in to cover the office the next day. Death had come so quickly in the night that there was no time to cancel the earliest appointments, and the elderly doctor was there to inform patients and handle emergencies. He told Richard that he didn't know what would become of the practice and gave him the phone number of the Fensters' friend, Dr. Harvey Neirman. Harvey contacted Mrs. Fenster at her parents' home and relayed to Richard that she would see him in the office after the memorial period.

Richard tells it, "When I arrived for the appointment the next week, the waiting room was empty, but through an open door into the examining room, I saw in a wall mirror the reflection of a twenty-five-year-old woman with a ponytail of beautiful red hair, and I was hooked."

I was once again the redhead in the mirror, but no longer wondering who I was.

I KEEP MY PROMISE

He popped up out of nowhere. That day. Harvey on the phone. Someone interested in the practice. Tell him I'll talk to him next week when *shivah* is over.

I didn't like him. How could I like anyone who'd sit in the doctor's chair and be irrefutable confirmation that Seymour was never coming back? More than a prospect, Richard was a threat.

He was different from Seymour in every way— medium height, wavy dark hair showing a few strands of premature grey, and a deeply intense expression. His clothes sat on him impeccably.

We didn't settle anything on the first visit. Richard went on to explore a practice in Windsor Locks that was longer established and making more money. But the sale price was higher, and Richard says he couldn't get my auburn ponytail out of his head. He came back, agreed to my asking price, and by the time we'd had several meetings with lawyers and signed the contracts for sale of the practice and lease of the space, I was getting more used to him and to my solo life. I began to recognize his infinite good nature and offbeat humor and to consider the possibility of Richard as a friend.

It was generally expected that the seller of a practice would write a letter to the patient base introducing the new doctor and encouraging their loyalty to him. This would be difficult for me because Seymour had been so widely loved. I met with Richard in the office a couple of times to draft a careful letter that wouldn't upset me or the patients. I entered in sadness but was surprised to walk out with my chin a little lifted from his sensitive and gently funny patter.

It's remarkable how my sunglasses began needing adjustment, first becoming too loose, then losing the pin in the temple altogether. Deciding I must have a new pair, Dick seated me in the examining chair and placed a tiny ruler across my nose to measure the distance between my pupils for fit. (I didn't know that this was totally unnecessary, since I needed no prescription in the glasses.) He lowered the ruler, frowned at it, and announced, "Hmm, you have no nose." It felt good to laugh.

On the rare times that I was on Market Square, I might pay a courtesy call to see how my tenant was prospering, and if he was not with a patient, we'd start to chat. One day the subject of weight came up. I confessed to having been fat till college. I laughed that on arrival in Boston, I'd still been wearing "slenderizing" dark clothing up to my neck and down to my wrists until my boyfriend Freddie's observation "You're not fat anymore" sent me to the petite shops for happier fashions.

Dick commented, "I note that you try to please those who care about you." I thought *Wow. I note that you hear more than I say.* Instead of dreading the sight of the office, I began to find there some small relief from heartache.

It was eerie. Dick had been raised in a rented flat very similar to my family's before his parents built their own home. He'd been a star Hebrew student and commiserated with my being denied a Bat Mitzvah. We'd both done well in school, but he'd left UConn, uncertain, to study optometry three months before I'd arrived there, uncertain what to study. Spookiest of all, his parents had been getting married in Boston on February 7, 1926, at the same time, during the same blizzard, as mine had been saying I Do in Hartford.

The firstborn of each marriage, Dick and Roan, arrived within eighteen days of each other two years later. No wonder one of us often nodded in recognition as the other told a story!

I still wanted to be a good daughter to the Fensters, and I drove to Lake Waubeka and to the Bronx to visit them as often as I could. Of course they weren't aware of the promise I'd made Seymour not to put my life on hold, yet on Father's Day when I kissed them goodbye, Mama murmured, "Next year you should come with a Friend." What generous permission!

Sometimes on a Sunday when I was the most down, the phone would ring and I'd hear Seymour's buddy Ted asking, "Are you alone? Would you like to come and have dinner with Ellen and me?" Oh, yes, I was so alone and so grateful for the rescue! When three months had passed and spring blossomed into summer, Ted and his wife also invited their single friend Irving to one of those dinners. Irving sold records to music stores and was very knowledgeable in the classics. He invited me to go with him in a few weeks to a Sunday concert of the Boston Symphony Orchestra at Tanglewood, their summer home in Lenox, Massachusetts. In this special place in the Berkshire Mountains, music lovers can either sit in the outdoor auditorium under a canopy, enjoy a picnic at a table on the surrounding grass, or spread a blanket and bask in the sun while listening to one of the world's greatest orchestras. It's about a two-hour drive from Hartford.

Umm, the invitation: I knew I'd promised Seymour, but I was caught off guard, and I wasn't ready. It had been two and a half years since I'd been on a date with anyone other than my husband. I was sure that Irving meant it only to be a friendly sharing of good music, but having just met him, I was uneasy. Still, he was a nice enough fellow, and I'd given my word to Seymour. I accepted the invitation gingerly. Then without warning, a strange thought came zinging out of left field: *Why Irving first and not Dick?*

Oh?

Well.

It was obviously time to check out sudden mysterious eye aches. As I sat in the examining chair the next day, Dick asked me as if on cue, "How are you?"

"Well, I'm a little nervous. I've just accepted a date to go to Tanglewood in a couple of weeks." He registered the information and kept checking out my eyes. What a surprise that he found nothing wrong with them! As I thanked him and was leaving, he said, "I hope you won't think me too forward, but if you're dating, I would like to take you out."

Demurely, I said, "I would like that." He got tickets to Oakdale Music Theater, a tent theater up the road in Wallingford, for that weekend. I was glad he was to be my first date the second time around.

It was baseball season, and on the way to our pre-theater dinner, Dick informed me, "I'm a big fan of Joe DiMaggio."

Sitting next to him in the car, wearing a delicate pastel print chiffon dress, I rejoined, "Oh, you're just a hero worshipper! Yogi Berra is as valuable to the Yankees as Joe." Dick's shaggy black eyebrows shot up, and he swiveled his head to look at me with a startled grin.

"Yogi Berra! What do you know about Yogi Berra?"

"I know he's a great clutch hitter." When Dick's eyes stretched as wide as his grin, I thought a silent *Thank you, brother Howard, for my valuable education*!

But baseball wasn't the only interest Dick and I shared. As we had more dates, we talked for hours about music, theater, religion, politics, the meaning of life and...and...and...We couldn't *stop* talking! I knew only a minimum about the visual arts, and Dick was as thorough a coach in that field as Howard had been in sports, taking me to museums and galleries, sharing art books, and giving me another lifetime gift.

Irving not only loved orchestral music but rejoiced as much as I in the sound of a sixteen-pound bowling ball rumbling down the polished wooden alley, ending in the crash of flying pins. Yet whatever I was doing, whoever I was with, there was always that tender spot, hiding from hurt, that belonged to Seymour Fenster. When, watching a play at Ivoryton Theater, Irving took my hand, I snatched it back as if I'd been burned. I continued to wear my wedding rings, and the first thing either fellow saw when he came to pick me up for a date was the framed photograph in my living room of my husband and me at our belated wedding reception.

Almost as soon as I'd returned to work at The Hartford in April, a flyer had been circulated offering employees an October group tour of Western Europe. The itinerary and price were tempting, and I'd thought it would be a welcome respite from six months on an emotional Cyclone. I'd signed up for it with three friends from the Girls Club.

Now October was here and the trip was proving to be the balm I'd hoped for...until I was stricken at St. Peter's Basilica in Rome. As I looked up at the painted canopy soaring over the magnificent central altar, the achingly beautiful, ethereal harmony of a mysterious hidden choir peeled away the careful protection from the still unhealed wound within me. I was left dangerously vulnerable. On the way out of the Basilica, our guide offhandedly pointed out, "To your left is the famous Pieta." There was then no barrier separating me from a marble Mary holding the limp crucified form of Jesus across her lap. Her left hand, with its helpless palm turned up, plaintively asked, "How could you do this to my son?" Yet it showed a resignation so pathetic that unguarded tears leapt down my face. What pain must Michelangelo have known to have sculpted such a hand! I knew that pain.

That week I wrote a postcard only to Irving. Sensing

that Dick was more seriously interested in me, I didn't want to encourage him by suggesting that I even thought of him while away. Yet once home, I was surprised to find myself disappointed when it was Irving who phoned the first day, while I waited, waited, waited for Dick to call. What if he had forgotten about me while I was gone? Maybe I should have mailed him a card. When his call a whole day later brought such relief, I could no longer tell myself that I wasn't ready.

As he picked me up for dinner on Saturday, my throat felt a little scratchy, and during the evening a wracking cough developed. Dick, his usual witty self, composed nonsense poetry to amuse me. When he began extolling a freckled flower in clever rhyme, laughing so hurt my throat that I asked him to take me home. Alone at my dining room table, drinking hot tea infused with brandy and honey, I smiled to think back on the truncated evening and how good it was to see him again.

What a juggling of emotions! In December it was time to order a headstone for Seymour's grave to be ready for unveiling on the April anniversary of his death. Sitting next to Dick in the darkness of the moving car one evening, out of the blue I began to sob without restraint, releasing the residue of sorrow that wouldn't stay buried. My companion was wise; he stopped the car at the side of the road, but he didn't make a move toward me. He sat there quietly and let me empty it all out. Only then was I able to make an appointment with the stonecutter and really move forward.

After that Dick asked me to save all my weekends for him, and Irving withdrew quietly. Dick had formed a warm friendship with Barney Wallace, owner of the shoe store on the corner of Market and Main in Newington. One night Barney and his wife Sue invited us for dinner. As we four retired to their living room after the meal, Barney put a record on the turntable. It was Carmina Burana, the cantata that had almost estranged me from Seymour three and a half years earlier! Dick, hearing it for the first time, GOT IT. He and I were lying on our stomachs on the carpet, a favorite listening position. Although we were several feet apart, Carl Orff's "sacred and profane" music charged the space between us with such an electric current that we were embarrassed to be in the presence of others.

I moved the reception portrait out of my living room, and I bought an inexpensive topaz ring to replace the wedding set on my left hand. This was the signal that Dick had been waiting for. After the unveiling the next April, he presented me with a new diamond for that finger.

LILY AND LOUIE

I must have been the kind of girl that boys bring home to their parents, 'cuz I sure did meet a passel of 'em. But Dick didn't bring me home on approval, like my mother did new clothes. Marriage was already in the air, and there was no question that he'd change his mind.

The day I met Lillian and Louis Lovins, I'd taken the train and subway into the Bronx to visit Seymour's family, and on the way back I left the train in Bridgeport. I knew Dick would be waiting on the platform when I emerged smartly dressed, even to a chic new hat. But I didn't see him. I waited patiently for a short while, and then thinking we might have got our signals mixed, I looked for him in the station. Not there. I was starting to feel a little panicked until I walked back out to the platform and saw him hurrying toward me. He'd been right there, right on time, but, he said, "I've never seen you in a hat before, and I must have walked right by you." I had no excuse for not spotting him.

As soon as we walked in the front door at 649 West Jackson Avenue, I felt the warmth and grace that filled that home. I was welcomed with generous hospitality and led through the tastefully furnished living room into the wood-paneled den. There, Dick's mother had set out crackers with her homemade chopped herring, a culinary masterpiece for which she was famous. His father asked what I would like to drink and made me a martini of perfect proportions.

While Lillian Lovins (later to be fondly known as Grammy Lily) put the finishing touches on dinner in the kitchen, I sat on a stepstool in the corner, chatting easily with her. She had already set a beautifully appointed table in the dining room and was so well organized in the kitchen that she declined my offers of help. I was spiritually and physically relaxed sitting on that stool with my feet tucked up under the first step, talking with a woman whom I quickly came to love. Once again there was a Judy's Corner that made me feel I belonged.

Short, busty, with softly coiffed pure white hair, Mom Lovins presented a comfortable appearance to go with her calm voice and demeanor. She was a spectacular traditional cook, and I first learned at her table that "kosher" and "gourmet" need not be mutually exclusive.

Louie Lovins was short, grey-haired and somewhat round. I felt his acceptance even while his wife was still troubled by my former elopement. Dad Lovins and I discovered that we both liked to try new and exotic foods, and on my first visit he offered to buy a tin of chocolate-covered ants if I'd join him in eating some. Well, we never went quite that far but always felt that adventurous kinship when the family dined out.

Dick's younger brother, Alan, was away for a year of postgraduate study in Germany, but after dinner the parents, Dick, and I gathered around the piano in the living room for their traditional family musicale. Mom Lovins sang soprano in their temple's choir and had considered a career as a concert pianist before having her family. As she played her first notes and we started to sing, she turned to me in surprise and exclaimed, "A soprano!" I teased her that where most mothers would have been happy with A Nice Jewish Girl, she was excited that her son brought home A Soprano. When Alan came home from Germany, he added his beautiful baritone voice to Dick's and Louie's to round out the family ensemble.

After a meeting with my mother, Lillian felt more comfortable about the circumstances of my first marriage. At 649 West Jackson Avenue she created a charming engagement party, rivaling any caterer's effort, to introduce me to family friends and Dick's crowd. The May Fourth Party has remained a cherished memory. Later in the month I met the rest of the family at a party at the home of his Aunt Ann and Uncle Max Toder in Malden, Massachusetts. It was marked by the same warmth and humor I'd encountered in Bridgeport. I knew I was a very lucky woman.

Dick and I were married on May 30, 1958. The Lovins and Horowitz parents became such good friends that they sometimes snuck off without us on little day trips. That completed our happiness.

SAFELY MARRIED

When I'd made my promise to Seymour, I didn't dream that I could love again so soon. I shared Mother's embarrassment about announcing my engagement a month after Seymour's unveiling, but I was twenty-six and Dick had just turned thirty. We didn't want to wait a year to begin a life together.

Although Jules, Hartford's popular kosher caterer, was booked solid for Sunday weddings from June till the end of the year, it struck me that we could sneak in ahead of the June crowd. May 30, 1958, was a Friday and Memorial Day. As long as we were out of the hall before the Sabbath started at sundown, we could be married that day, and our Massachusetts and New York relatives would have the holiday off to travel. A favorite young uncle of Dick's was a baker in New York, and Sunday being his busiest day, he could never attend family weddings. If Dick and I were married on a Friday afternoon, even Uncle Harry could be there!

Weekday and Memorial Day lunchtimes not being in demand for caterers, Jules was available. He'd just ended his long association with the Shangri-La restaurant downtown, and our ceremony would be the first in his own sparkling new Maison de Jules in the north end.

I felt so bad that my parents had not had the fun of planning my first wedding that I was happy to have them make this one. I asked Mother to come with me to shop for my dress.

I had never dreamed of an elaborate white gown with a trailing train. I couldn't understand spending a lot of money on something that would have to be cleaned, special-wrapped, and stored for eternity after only one wearing. The same money could buy so many lasting things to establish a home! Anyway, ours was to be a small wedding with only fifty family members and closest friends, who didn't need to be impressed.

Mother agreed about the white gown, but once again we had dueling visions. While I was thinking *bride*, she was thinking *widow*. In her mind that meant sophistication. She pulled a chocolate brown chemise off the rack, but I'd waited too long for a slender figure to wear that year's distorting fashion. And although I wasn't eligible for symbolic white, brown was absolutely morose!

Mother remained stuck in Second Wedding mode until I reminded her that this was the first wedding for Dick and his family and that they were entitled to something pretty, happy, and full of hope. I selected a moderately-priced pink chiffon dress with flared mid-calf skirt and embroidery at the sweetheart neckline and hem. To my relief, Mother's eyes lit up as she realized, "Of course! You're still a young girl!" She was even delighted with my choice of white linen high heels dotted with pink and red rosebuds, reminiscent of my grandmother's missing fan and the vetoed bedroom wallpaper of so many years before.

But the poor woman was trying to abide by her notion of a discreet event only a year after a death, and she regressed. Forgetting about the "young girl," she informed me that she and Dad felt music would be inappropriate. None would be booked.

I saw the way the wind was blowing and asked, "Would you like me to wear a black armband walking down the aisle?" That shocked her into conceding that after all, a small combo might play just for the processional, recessional and one traditional dance of bride and groom, maybe even joined by the four parents.

"And how will you announce to our guests, who've given up their day and driven in from out of state, that they are not even to step foot on the dance floor to celebrate with us?"

With continuing encouragement, Mother was slowly able to open her hand to let go of death, and our wedding emerged fully joyous, complete with a life-affirming horah. A finally smiling, seated Mother and Dad were circled, crowned with wreaths, and hoisted high on their chairs by the carefree dancing guests, as Jewish parents are entitled to be when they marry off their last child.

Dick had declined to meet the Fensters as Mama had suggested the year before. I was outvoted on inviting them to our wedding, and, excluded, although Seymour's folks said they were glad for me, they did not otherwise acknowledge this marriage. Eighteen months later, when I was newly pregnant, they wrote to ask if they could move Seymour's grave from the quiet grassy hill where he rested to an overcrowded urban cemetery in the Bronx where phalanxes of somber grey headstones contested for room. As much as I hated that vision, I saw that it was now right for him to be near them, and I agreed. But as the day approached, my pregnancy showed frightening signs of trouble, and my obstetrician forbade me to attend the disinterment or reburial. Though I ruefully explained this to the Fensters, after a short exchange of letters, my contact with the family was broken. It was never my desire or intention. Their last letters came addressed to "Mrs. Judy" with no last name. I was sad for them that they could not remember or bear to use it. I no longer bore their name.

I was now Judy Lovins.

There!

THE GAMBLE

Voluptuous clouds of bright pink blossoms were massed on the spreading branches of the crabapple tree. Behind them, the pale grey house barely peeked out like a demure maiden hiding behind a lavish fan. As I stepped from the realtor's car in the well-kept neighborhood that day in May,1967 I told her, "I can't see the house, but I'll take the tree."

The back yard was no less appealing. The boundary at the end of a grassy expanse was Trout Brook, which gurgled and giggled, trying to cheer up the willow whose weeping branches drooped down to the high bank. Half way between the house and the brook stood two sentinel apple trees, their branches meeting across an open space between their trunks. I pictured my children enjoying the same fun I'd had as a child climbing a neighbor's apple tree.

Hugging the house on the back and south sides, tall fragrant lilac bushes lured an occasional hummingbird, and from the base of the garage, lilies of the valley broadcast their loud aroma. Near the unfenced border between the house and its neighbor to the south, a lacy African sumac tree promised shade for our picnic table.

But we hadn't yet seen the inside! Leaving a modern split-level house in a development, we were enchanted by the traditional center-entrance Colonial with three large bedrooms and bath upstairs. From the top of the stairs I could look down through the high windows in the front door and see beyond the crabapple blooms to the modest houses across the street, each with its own distinct character.

Downstairs the living room was big enough for our console piano, and a generous lilac-ringed screened porch sat behind it in the midst of pastel fragrance. Windows in perpendicular walls of the wainscoted dining room filled the space with light, and between them a built-in, glass-fronted corner cabinet stood waiting for our small collection of cut crystal. Off the large eat-in kitchen (alas, without a dishwasher) a laundry/mud room gave in the front onto a little square porch at the top of a few stairs to the driveway and in back to an even smaller porch atop another few to the back yard.

Not only was the Fernwood area of West Hartford charming, but Morley School, like the rest of the town's schools, had a glowing reputation for providing a superior education. It was about a mile from the house we were looking at. Since our petite Susie was to start kindergarten in the fall, Dick walked with her to the school while I followed slowly in the car to see if she could cover the distance without difficulty. She could, and we bought the house.

We moved in on August 12, 1967. Dick built a platform next to the back porch for our trash barrels, and one autumn day I found a lovely little decorator pillow sitting on top of one of those barrels. I surmised that the kids had been using it in some play activity and canvassed our neighbors to see who owned it. Nobody claimed the cushion, but one woman guessed that a raccoon who habituated the brook might have appropriated it from a barrel further up the street, carried it through the unfenced yards and abandoned it when he saw something more interesting in ours.

We were introduced to more Trout Brook wildlife as the seasons progressed. On a winter night when we heard a rattling out back, I put on the porch light and through the glass storm door found myself eye to black-masked eye with a four-legged visitor. I was surprised to see him when there was snow on the ground, but our Encyclopedia Britannica revealed that although raccoons sleep a lot in the cold weather, they do not hibernate. Indeed they mate in winter, with a gestation period of sixty-three days. I began counting. Sure enough, just after two months of quiet on the back porch we heard a commotion again. The mother was sitting in a barrel stuffing trash morsels into her mouth while two or three babies went tumbling down the stairs. Incensed, I yelled at her, "Never mind feeding your fat face; take care of your babies before they get hurt!"

Another Trout Brook denizen came visiting that spring. As snowmelt came down the Connecticut River and its tributaries, the brook flooded our yard up to the apple trees. When the water receded, we looked out Mike's bedroom window and saw an unsightly mole lumbering across the mud that was left. Dick located the hole from which he'd emerged and placed a smoke bomb in it. We felt bad, but we'd spent much money and effort on the lawn and didn't want it full of mole holes. We just wanted the animal to move on.

By the next year I'd read Wind in the Willows to the children. (Its words are delicious on the tongue! I savored each one I read aloud, and I never would have believed a book could TASTE that good!) Now we could more correctly identify the long, skinny-tailed visitor to our flooded yard as Ratty, and we fondly welcomed him. This time we left him alone, knowing he would wend his way back to the bank of the brook and from there out of our lives for another year. When the grass grew back, it was lush from the flooding and suffered no harm from our friend the water rat.

Not everything came *out* of the brook. Sometimes things went *in*, like Susie's friend Ann. In midwinter the girls were playing out back in their warm coats, boots, and mittens. I was in the comfortably heated house in just a cotton housedress without a sweater. I was bare-legged in slippers. Suddenly Susie rushed into the house. "Mommy! Ann fell in the brook and can't get out!" I tore out the door "as is" and raced across the yard. With my first steps I realized that rain had frozen on top of deep snow and formed a hard crust. At full tilt, my every footfall was plunging through the crust, cutting my bare legs like a razor. But I couldn't stop. At the flowing brook I found Ann had tried to pull herself up onto land, but the bank was too slippery. I realized that I, too, might slide in and do neither of us any good. In my cotton dress I flopped onto my stomach on the crusted snow and reached out my hand, feeling as if I were in a movie. Ann held on, and I slid her up across the glaze into the level yard. Lighter in weight and wearing boots, she got to the house without being cut, and luckily, the bloody crisscrosses up and down my legs healed before long without leaving scars.

New fauna arrived not only by water but by air. Dick helped six-year-old Mike build a small bird feeder and affix it outside his bedroom window. When birds dined at the upstairs feeder, seeds spilled into the channel of the kitchen storm window directly below it. Every day while I did dishes at the sink in front of that window, a black-capped chickadee hung upside down from the sash and periodically dipped down to retrieve a meal from the channel. Watching him was so much fun that I almost didn't miss the dishwasher.

The cardinals who perched on the lilacs were better parents than the greedy raccoon in the trash barrel. One spring day I noticed the soft brown female sitting on a lilac bush out back with three of her youngsters. She hopped off a low branch onto the ground, then back to the branch. The young birds copied the action. After several repetitions, suddenly a brilliant red male whizzed in out of nowhere. This was apparently the poppa, because I could almost hear him scolding, "Why are you coddling these kids? What's with the short hops to the ground? Children, this is how to

FLY!" And he swooped the length of the yard from the lilacs to the willow, then came back and practically pushed the kids off the branch. They all made it to the willow and back, and I felt so privileged to have witnessed the flying lesson!

When Dick and I decided to move the air-conditioner from the front window of our bedroom around the corner to the side, we bracketed it and lifted it slowly. To our astonishment, between the bottom of the unit and the sloping sill of the window a family of teeny naked birds sat in a nest alone. Holding our breath, we slowly, gently, put the unit back. We hoped that returning parents wouldn't realize that humans had come in contact with the nest and therefore abandon their featherless babies. Quickly agreeing not to move the air-conditioner until those kids were established, we became almost adoptive parents, gratefully eavesdropping from our bed on daily chirpings, eventual flying lessons, and then silence. Only when we were sure the family had left the nest did we move the unit.

In addition to our bird and animal friends, we were delighted with our new neighbors. Right next door Ned Brewer with sons Steven and Eddie wasted no time in welcoming Mike and Dick into the active Indian Guides program for hours of father/son fun. Although my amply feathered Big Buffalo and Black Buffalo became members of the Brewers' Hopi tribe, I told them I wanted to buy some Micmac and Nipmuk knickknacks from other tribes. I challenged them to repeat my order fast without stumbling. Almost fifty years later one of us will still test our tongue-twister skill and rouse a family laugh.

Patty Brewer and Susie became fast friends. The girls looked adorable marching around in their mothers' old clothes, high heels, jewelry, and accessories. Yes, I'd saved my cast-offs for my daughter to play in. The girls added their own giggles. At Christmastime our children were invited to help the Brewers decorate their tree, and in the fall their kids helped hang colorful gourds and corn husks on the screened porch where we ate our Sukkot meals. There were five Brewer young 'uns in all, and we often hosted an impromptu one-base softball game in our yard. To improve his fielding, little Tommy Brewer would ask Dick to "bat me a high fwy, Mister Wubbins." It is surprising how often one of our family members can still find a way to inject that lisped phrase into a family conversation!

Up and down Montclair Drive and in the wider neighborhood were other bright, pleasant companions for both parents and children. It wasn't long before Mike's Blue X Club was meeting in our back yard, the young pirates sailing on the tire swing we'd hung from the willow and escaping along the banks of the brook. Scouts hiding in the apple trees followed them through spyglasses.

Susie found a haven from summer's heat in her reading tree. She could easily raise her short legs to the low crotch in the birch next to the crabapple tree and climb up to sit with a book in the V between two higher branches. A muffin pan wedged securely on an adjacent leafy elbow held a snack and cold drink. There she spent hours hidden away above the front yard, happily reading.

Morley School was a jewel. Both Mike and Susie had been introduced to education in Mrs. Dougherty's private preschool in Newington, where that loving lady wiped up an accidental Spilly Willie with an understanding hug instead of a reprimand. Mike had finished kindergarten in the Newington school right near our house. Then in West Hartford, Morley gradually integrated its kindergartners a few at a time over the space of a couple of weeks, affording Susie individual attention and tender concern that would follow the class all the way up through sixth grade.

Education there wasn't static. When Mike was in fourth grade, a new system was adopted for his age group whereby each morning students scheduled themselves into their day's classes by dropping punch cards into appropriate slots. No one led them *en masse* through the halls, but each was expected to be where he belonged at the self-appointed time. Some of the kids goofed off in the TV "lab" when they were expected in an academic class, but Mike came home with a big grin one day and exulted, "I just love being responsible!" In addition to knowing his material, could we ask for anything more?

We could.

On the morning of Mike's seventh birthday he complained that his legs hurt. Thinking he was over-excited about his party that afternoon, we joked about growing pains arriving with his new age. But it wasn't growing pains. It became acute grownup agony. During three tortured months when Dick and I begged a series of specialists for a diagnosis and heard them misread X-rays and bark up one wrong tree after another, the pain in Mike's monstrous swollen knee and opposite ankle made walking a nightmare. He negotiated the stairs to his bedroom "by fanny," sitting on a low step and hitching his butt up to sit on the next higher one till he reached the top. At school his math teacher confessed to barely holding back tears while watching him painfully hoist himself up to the second floor by the bannister. But there was still no diagnosis.

There was no more apple-tree climbing for him. The kind Blue X boys stationed their pal on the ground as a special scout, slowly delivering coded messages between the trunks and over to the willow.

One day when there was no school or doctor's appointments, I took Mike with me to the Head Start venue where I volunteered. In a room full of children, crafts and playthings, he sat alone in a chair as still as a statue, eyes straight ahead. It hurt too much to turn his newly stiff neck. Pleading "Help us!" Dick and I took him the next day to Newington Children's Hospital, where he was summarily, with no gentle orientation, put to bed flat on his back. He spent the next week there starting treatment for juvenile rheumatoid arthritis, which slowly conquered his pain. The rheumatologist said he'd outgrow the arthritis in six months to seven years. He was wrong.

Every day in the hospital I read to Mike. Strangely, there were almost never other daytime visitors in his ward, and the first time I started a book, I noticed that all the other young boys leaned forward in their beds to hear me. The Legg Perthes patients rolled across the floor on their platforms to form a circle around us. All week I kept my voice up so that they all could hear, and I showed illustrations all around the ward. Distracting those captive kids was one of the most rewarding experiences of my life.

Mike was discharged from the hospital with instructions to remain bedridden for another six weeks. He was allowed to sit up in bed but was forbidden to even dangle his legs over the side. Before Mike came home, Dick and I moved his bed and his bookcase full of toys and reading matter downstairs into a bright corner of the living room so that he would not be isolated. An adjacent play table held meals, games, and craft supplies. Morley School briefly sent a tutor before determining that Mike was so advanced in his work that he had already effectively completed first grade. Susie spent many hours playing with her brother before joining her friends outside. After school many of his friends came by. His grandparents and some of our own friends visited, and a flood of mail poured in. I played countless games of checkers with my son, and he and his daddy spent many pleasant evening hours together in that activity corner.

When the six weeks were up, Mike was allowed to rise from his bed and, although still limping, attend day camp at the superb West Hartford Children's Museum. When he came home the first day glowing about the fun and learning he'd enjoyed, Dick and I were enormously grateful that such a happy experience would cap his summer. But when we heard that the group was to sleep outdoors in the park one night, we teetered between wanting with all our hearts for him to share in the fun and fearing that the cold air and hard ground would reactivate his arthritis.

Mike's counselor confided that because his own son was blind, he knew how to discreetly watch over a child with a problem. He told us no contact sports were planned that were forbidden to Mike, and that he would make sure that our son took his aspirin as prescribed. Reassured for the moment, we sent Mike off with a plastic shower curtain for a ground cloth and a brand new, warm sleeping bag. Dick and I did not sleep that night. We sat on the living room sofa holding hands, asking ourselves if we were despicable parents to let our arthritic son sleep on the cold ground. We were terrified that we had done the wrong thing and set our child back.

Since Dick had patients in the morning, I went to pick Mike up by myself with great guilt and trepidation. Would our son be all right? I had not long to wait for my answer. He spotted the car right away and came RUNNING to greet me, an ecstatic grin covering his face! RUNNING! I had not seen him run for almost six months. I blinked back any tears that would embarrass him and managed to match his grin as he walked without a limp to the car. I quietly but fervently thanked his counselor for his care. On the way home I joyfully listened to Mike's animated reliving of the great time he'd had, and the minute we got home I called to tell Dick the amazing news.

For the second time in my life, I had to suspect that having fun is a more powerful medicine than we understand. At Mike's next checkup with the rheumatologist, I asked how he could explain that his patient had started running and walking normally after a night sleeping on the ground. With a somber frown, Dr. Sourpuss answered, "I don't recommend it."

There were short relapses. Over two summers I noted that fewer attacks came than during the winters. When I inquired, two consultants separately told me that moving to a warm, dry climate would be of no help and would only disrupt the whole family.

During that time Dick sold his optometric practice, as he had planned, and finished all graduate course work at the University of Connecticut to become a clinical psychologist. He was still writing his Ph.D. dissertation when, at the end of his internships, he was offered enviable positions at Yale's Child Guidance Center and in the West Hartford and Simsbury school systems. With what pride he would have accepted them! I had become Susie's Brownie leader, and when our active troop's agenda came to the notice of the Scout organization, I was asked to become organizer for all the neighborhood Brownie troops. Because I have great respect for the Girl Scout organization, I would have loved that! Mike and Susie were both doing well in school, and we'd made many good friends at Newington's Temple Sinai. There was so much to look forward to!

But we were helpless to fend off our child's recurring bouts of pain. Once when Dick was carrying him into the doctor's office to have his knee drained and cortisone injected yet again, Mike asked, "Daddy, why does it have to hurt so much?" It was only with great difficulty that Dick held himself together.

Finally I pinned down that doctor: "Please listen to me without bias. Given that my husband is starting a new career and it doesn't matter where he starts it, given that we are a close family and make friends easily, disregarding any feared disruption, how many chances in ten are there that Mike would do better in a warm, dry place?"

Since it was the only stone we'd left unturned, if he said one or two I was prepared to start packing. He said four. And then suddenly Mike's shoulder went stiff. As the doctor administered yet another cortisone shot, he told Dick that Mike might not ever again be able to raise that arm over his head. In less than two months Dick secured a rewarding position in Phoenix, Arizona, and we moved to our new home in the city on the desert.

When we arrived in July 1971 our son immediately became more mobile. The first time I lifted his jeans into the washing machine and saw both knees dirty, my eyes brimmed with grateful tears. When I watched him climb a hill, I quietly cried again. And as Mike's shoulder quickly regained full range of motion, Dick wiped away tears of relief. The arthritis went into total remission for two years. It now appears rarely and briefly, and he manages it without disrupting his life.

Mike is comfortable living in Arizona as the head of his own family. Even though Sue's life script led her back to the East Coast with her husband and children, she and Mike remain warm, close buddies through modern technology and periodic in-person visits.

When we were preparing to leave New England, I couldn't conceive of living so far from the ocean. Yet almost as soon as we landed in Arizona, I fell in love with an entity just as vast and captivating. The desert, with its exquisite flora, scenic mountains, and expansive vistas makes time seem to stretch as broad as space. I understood quickly that I had arrived where I was meant to be.

Our family gave up much to move, but we gained much. Though we didn't win one hundred percent, we had to take the gamble.

FREEING MOLLIE

Although she didn't make it as a nurse, to confront her panoply of phobias and function as wife, mother-through-great-grandmother, parolee mentor, air raid warden, Girl Scout leader, super saleslady, and cross-country traveler, Mollie Horowitz has had to be a gutsy lady.

When, after moving to the quiet suburb of West Hartford in 1955, she began experiencing one niggling ailment after another, she understood that she had to change more than her address. Before the Crash she'd helped out in Dad's dress shop, and they'd learned that they had their remarkable sales ability in common. Many years later she'd had fun working at the S & A on Saturdays. Yet at this late stage, Dad wouldn't hear of her putting that skill to use again; people would think he couldn't support his wife. But she knew what she needed. One day she walked a couple of miles uphill and along a boulevard to Lord & Taylor department store. When Dad came home she told him she'd been hired as a part-time sales associate, and the discussion was closed.

In 1963 my father collapsed suddenly after zestfully partaking of abundant fare at a friend's dinner party, leaving his fearful/brave wife single for the next twenty-two years. After sitting *shivah* at Roan's, the first thing Mother did was to move out of the house she'd shared with Dad into a garden apartment near Ro. As she required, it had its own outside entrance so that she need fear no stranger walking down an enclosed hall past her door.

My sixty-year-old mother then bought a car and learned to drive so that she wouldn't burden her daughters and could easily get to the job she loved. She passed her licensing test on the first try, and behind the wheel she was no little old lady in tennis shoes. Though she wouldn't enter a major highway, on surface roads she was as competent at driving as at her other endeavors. I was surprised to feel perfectly comfortable as her passenger, and I complimented her for it.

Mother felt abandoned when married friends stopped inviting her to their social gatherings. I observed her disappointment and made a note never to do that, not only because of its cruelty but because I knew that I'd deprive myself of half the interesting people in the world. So what if there's an odd number of guests at the dinner table? Mother rescued her feelings by finding new friends among other widows and enjoying frequent lunch dates and long phone calls with them.

At Lord & Taylor, she impressed customers by accurately computing in her head the total cost of multiple items plus tax long before she got to the cash register. She enjoyed selling folks things they wanted until thrice-weekly dialysis, unreliable legs, and moving to assisted living in Newington ended her career at age eighty. At her new home she quickly led a revolt of the residents against the dining room food and got the menu improved. When friends picked her up for lunch outside Jefferson House, the home added new restaurants that she discovered to its destinations for weekly outings. She'd agree to roll from her room to their bus in a wheelchair, but at the other end she insisted on stiffening her will and walking upright into the restaurant. That was Mollie!

When my family moved to Phoenix in 1971, I was concerned how Mother would get to Michael's Bar Mitzvah thirty-two months later and Susan's Bat Mitzvah nineteen months after that. Mother was afraid of airplanes. Each year after she and Dad motored down to Miami Beach to visit her brothers, she declined to board a puddle jumper to the Havana casinos. How would she ever get cross-country for these momentous family events? I needn't have worried. When the time came, she flew. After Mike's Bar Mitzvah she stayed with us for a month, and then she flew back to Connecticut alone. Once that hurdle was cleared, she returned for a month every year until her health forbade.

I was working mornings in Scottsdale. On week days I'd drop Mother off first at Fashion Square, where she browsed the fine department stores using her Lord & Taylor reciprocal discount. When she tired, she found a seat in Dillard's shoe department and people-watched till I picked her up. On my bowling night, my Non-Smoking League mates showered her with attention. She had never been in a bowling alley, never heard the glorious sound of a strike, and couldn't take her eyes off the action. On the way home, she presented me with the most precious gift of a lifetime:

"I like the way you live," she said. "You're fun. I wish I'd understood you better when you were a child."

Oh, Mother, I wish I'd better understood your frustrations when I was struggling to separate from you.

It's now 1976. She's seventy-five years old, and Dick and I are taking her to Disneyland. On the way to L.A., we stop overnight in our favorite Palm Springs motel. Because Mom feels unsafe alone in a single room, we're splurging on a twenty-eight-dollar luxury suite where she has her own room within our locked door, and we can even prepare kosher food for her in our kitchen.

After the six-hour drive across the desert, we can't wait to introduce her to the motel's courtyard hot tub. It will be a new experience for her. But when she tells us she'll be content to sit on the pool deck and watch us soak, I realize that my modest mother doesn't own a swimsuit to swap for her dress and pantyhose. I look around. It's midday and there's not another soul in sight.

"I want you to experience the feeling," I urge. "You don't need to sit in the spa. Just take off your hose, come sit on the deck and at least put your legs in to feel the whirlpool action."

"No," she says, "I'm fine." Oh, Lord, how many times have I heard that in a lifetime? I can't stand watching her perched straight-backed on the foot of a chaise. I have a wild idea. (Am I not a *vilda chaya*?)

"Mom," I begin, "It's such a hot day, if you get your hose wet, they'll dry before we get back to the room..." To my joy, she agrees to remove her high heels, sit on the deck with her dress just above her knees and let her legs down into the spa, still encased in nylon. As the water swirls around them, I see her whole body soften and a Cheshire cat smile spread over her face. I feel it mirrored on mine.

On our way into town, Mom had spotted the fake black-and-white cow standing on a second-floor balcony above Swiss Chalet's patio dining. This woman, who must never directly ask for anything on pain of losing her Jewish Mother license, had blurted out, "Can we eat supper there?" Of course, we will dine nowhere else! Although she won't eat non-kosher meat, the fun décor makes her fish dinner the tastiest she's ever had.

For Mom's comfort, I've included only Disneyland's tamest attractions on our itinerary while still trying to give her the flavor of the place. Our first stop the next day is the terrace where we're each lunching on a plate of three round pancakes poured and decorated to look like Mickey Mouse's head with two big, round ears. They make her laugh. While we're eating, the Mark Twain steamboat sails around the bend, its lively whistle tooting as it pulls into the dock near us. The sound transforms my mother into a wide-eyed youngster, and excitedly she asks, "Are we going on that?"

Startled, I ask in return, "WOULD you go on that?"

She answers, "I will go on anything you think is fun!" My being fills with light, laughter, and wonder to see my lifelong opponent emancipating! I mentally shred the plans I've so carefully written, and we head for the steamboat dock to buy tickets.

Boarding the boat, I stay very close to Mother in case I need to put my arms firmly around her trembling body as I did at Grand Canyon viewing platforms. But she heads straight for the railing and exuberantly exclaims as we glide by fanciful Disney attractions.

Dare we? Several years ago a young cousin joined our family's outing to the Magic Kingdom. A native Californian, she'd been there many times before, but she panicked as we approached the Pirates of the Caribbean ride. We'd never been on it, but viewing the long lines of kids eager to get in, we couldn't imagine what could have so terrified this child. I have my own hang-ups, but that day the kaleidoscopic wonder of the underground spectacle crowded them out. Now I warn Mother that although the three of us would be sitting together, the ride begins in the dark with a sudden steep drop down a flume and at the bottom, riding along on water, we'd be in the middle of a loud armed battle robustly enacted around us.

Her response: "Do you think it's fun?"

In answer, I can only repeat her incredulous exclamations as we whoosh down that inky incline: "How can I tell anyone about this?" She's high with delight! She's a happy little girl, gurgling, "How can I tell my friends what this is like? How can I describe what I'm doing?" At the bottom, amid all the furor and fire as pirates and sailors cross our bow with cutlasses flashing, her eyes and her smile are lit up like a party.

Fun? There is no greater fun than watching a phobic, straight-laced seventy-five-year-old lady immerse herself in a magical world and slough off her fears and obediently learned lifetime restraints.

And realizing that you really do love her.

Epilogue

FREEING JUDY

I began this memoir as the story of my quest for freedom to be myself. When I was done I realized that there were no villains or heroes in my story, only human beings who, while supposing we were doing our best, inevitably made mistakes that hurt other people.

It surprised me to realize that I had been collecting resentments. Since I have no room for resentments any longer, I decided to have a spiritual yard sale and dispose of any feelings that have no current value. The writing helped me to *just let it go*. I have sincerely forgiven anyone— especially the principal characters here—who ever offended or hurt me. With greater difficulty, I have even forgiven myself for hurt I caused others through my own insensitivity to their needs. This has brought true freedom that I never even knew to strive for! Now when I happen to catch sight of that redhead in the mirror, I can give her a little wink.

Acknowledgments

ACKNOWLEDGMENTS

This labor of love was only possible because of the selfless and limitless patience and partnership of my husband Dr. Richard Lovins. Thank you, Honey, for all the meals you prepared, dishes you washed, reading of each piece as it came off the printer, and your honest and helpful discussion.

My sister Roan Wetstone was always there on the other end of the phone to answer questions, share recollections, supply missing pieces, and offer such enthusiastic encouragement that she became a strong incentive to finish the job. In addition to being an enormous help, it's been as much fun working with her as it was to play together growing up.

My son Michael Lovins put up with his cyber-idiot mother with patience, good will, and his clever, stress-busting humor. He was an incalculable help in my struggle to feed my precious memories into the maw of the computer and move them on from there. His son Alex also humored his grandmother with valuable digital help. My daughter Dr. Sue Eick provided technical and spiritual support, not to mention her special brand of humorous respite, cross-country by phone and e-mail, and in personal visits.

I'm grateful to Dr. Alan Lovins for helping with my imperfect understandings of Judaism while respecting my feelings about how I sometimes personally experienced its actual practice.

Great thanks are due to all the members of the Ahwatukee Recreation Center Writers Group, whose comments, chuckles, and occasional empathetic tear kept me going. Special thanks to Rick Rolfe, my fellow Connecticut Yankee, for his understanding of the territory and his time-consuming help on the computer, and to memoir teacher Sue Cahill for her welcome and gently offered teachings and comments.

Warm hugs to Bob and Jean Hadley for being special, encouraging friends and for driving us all over Newington to share memories and take pictures.

Thank you to Arielle Eckstut and David Henry Sterry, authors of The Essential Guide to Getting Your Book Published, for their interest and advice. To Gayle Shanks of Changing Hands Bookstore for her personal interest and encouragement. To Dema Lee, author of Indian Oasis, for sharing information about publishing. To Rachel Winheld, Robin Wendehack, Dr. Lori Rand, Lorraine Rice, and Bob Stock for giving their time to read pieces of my offerings and make valuable suggestions.

Gratitude beyond expressing to Judith Thompson, editor, who taught me so much about writing—my writing in particular—and who, happily, became a warm friend beyond our professional relationship.

And bless Betts McCalla, publisher of Running Quail Press, for giving so freely of her delightful personal warmth in addition to her professional expertise. It was always so comfortable to work with her.

Lastly, apologies and thanks to all our neglected friends and relatives who were understanding and forgiving while I was preoccupied giving birth to this baby. I look forward to spending more time with you all now that it's seen the light of day.

9 780984 033164